CLIMBING HIGHER

Also by Msgr. David Rosage

Speak, Lord, Your Servant Is Listening
Listen to Him
The Bread of Life
A Lenten Pilgrimage
Follow Me

Climbing Higher

Reflections for
Our Spiritual Journey

David E. Rosage

SERVANT BOOKS
Ann Arbor, Michigan

Dedication

*To all my fellow travellers who not only
accompany me, but also support and
encourage me on my pilgrimage to the Father*

CONTENTS

Introduction

WE ARE A PILGRIM PEOPLE, members of a pilgrim church journeying back to our heavenly Father. Life is not merely an exile, nor is it a static state of rest and relaxation. It is not simply marking time. Life is dynamic, zestful, expansive — always moving forward. Life is a spiritual journey.

Mountains, from Sinai to Calvary, are prominently featured in God's dealing with his people. Mountaintops are a favorite trysting place of the Lord with his people. On our journey through life we figuratively climb many mountains and there have our peak experiences.

With the Israelites we have been freed from the slavery of sin by the cleansing waters of baptism — our Red Sea experience. In the desert we are conditioned and transformed as we spend time alone listening to the Lord in prayer.

On Mount Sinai we discover a Father who loves us just as we are.

On Mount Nebo we gaze longingly into the Promised Land and make our decision to cross the Jordan.

On the Mount of Beatitudes we listen to Jesus set forth a challenging lifestyle for us to follow.

On Mount Tabor we witness his majestic splendor in his yes to the Father.

On Mount Zion at the Last Supper Jesus confides to us: "I have greatly desired to eat this Passover with you before I suffer" (Lk 22:15).

Jesus appreciates our companionship as he trudges his painful way to Calvary.

Mary, our Mother, takes us by the hand as she ascends every height to which the Lord has called her.

Jesus awaits us at the end of our pilgrimage to present us to our gracious Father in an embrace of love which is infinite and eternal.

Scripture records accounts of many pilgrim-journeys. Abraham and Sarah set out from their homeland not knowing where the Lord was leading them. The Israelites, with Moses as their leader, set out on an uncharted journey of faith for forty years through the desert, hoping to reach a Promised Land. Mary and Joseph also made a pilgrimage of faith to Bethlehem, into exile in Egypt, and back to the hill country of Galilee, not knowing what kind of reception they would receive or what the Lord was going to ask of them next.

Our Mountain Climbing

The history of God dealing with his people forms a pattern for what he wishes in our lives. Life is a continual mountain climbing. As we ascend, with our vision fixed on the top of the mountain, a new vista is revealed to us and we seem to encounter God more easily. Our myopic vision expands into a more cosmic, panoramic view.

At the same time, many of our worldly interests become more peripheral. Each climb challenges us to fuller commitment, fuller involvement with the Lord. The reward is an expanded horizon, tasting anew the beauties of God's creation.

Each time we climb a spiritual mountain a transformation takes place. We grow and mature spiritually.

Our pilgrimage is intended to be a prayerful experience. The immanence of the Lord becomes more and more apparent as we leave the valleys of false allurements and distractions.

Our pilgrimage is a walk in faith. Our course may seem uncharted at times, which causes us to trust in the Creator of the mountains. We learn total dependence on our gracious Father.

Mountain climbing is purifying. We carry only essentials. We rid ourselves of all the excess baggage which clutters our life, in order to have greater mobility along life's journey.

This book endeavors to traverse in spirit the journey of the Chosen People of the Old Testament as well as the devoted disciples who followed Jesus. We listen to the call of Jesus to "come and see," so that we may have the inspiration, courage, and endurance to climb every mountain with him.

Hopefully these pages will contribute a little incentive to make our journey a more joyous one, filled with challenge, expectancy, and peace. May our joy brighten and lighten the journey of our fellow travellers as well.

The risen Jesus is walking with us as he walked with the disciples on the road to Emmaus. May he also keep our hearts burning within us as he reveals his Word to us.

"Come, then! Let us be on our way." (Jn 14:31)

ONE

Waters of Freedom

You brought them in and planted them on the mountain of your inheritance—the place where you made your seat, O Lord, the sanctuary, O Lord, which your hands established.

(Ex 15:17)

IN THESE WORDS from the Song of Moses after the Israelites had crossed the Red Sea, our loving Father is inviting us to recall and reflect, to pause and ponder his sustaining, providential love for us. Like the Israelites we are on a pilgrimage to the Promised Land —our union of love with our Father.

The Father's providential care for us encourages us to continue our pilgrimage with renewed perseverance.

God invites us to climb his mountain, to be alone with him frequently, to contemplate his leading us back to him.

Recall that during the time of a great famine the Israelites migrated to Egypt as their only hope of survival (Gn 46). At first they were well received because of their brother Joseph. But as time went on they were enslaved by the Egyptians, who resented and feared them (Ex 1).

As conditions of slavery worsened, they cried out to the Lord to save them from such inhuman treatment. God heard the distressing cry of his oppressed people. He freed them from their slavery and led them out into the desert where he would form them into his Chosen People. "You shall be my people and I will be your God" (Jer 30:22).

God would watch over them, protect them, and provide for them every step of the way.

> The Lord preceded them, in the daytime by means of a column of cloud to show them the way, and at night by means of a column of fire to give them light. Thus they could travel both day and night. Neither the column of cloud by day nor the column of fire by night ever left its place in front of the people.
>
> (Ex 13:21–22)

To reach Sinai the Israelites had to cross the Red Sea (or Reed Sea). Humanly speaking this was impossible. By this time the Egyptian army was in full pursuit to herd them back to slavery. In desperation the Israelites complained to Moses: "Were there no burial places in Egypt that you had to bring us out here?... Far better for us to be the slaves of the Egyptians than to die in the desert." (Ex 14:11–12)

The cry of these fleeing Israelite echoes our own. They lacked faith and trust in a God they hardly knew. They feared the risk of following him, of being annihilated by the approaching Egyptian army. They would have settled again for the slavery of Egypt and the fleshpots it provided. They had yet to experience the protecting, providential love of their caring God.

The slavery of sin can seem more satisfying to us, too, than the risk of turning to God and to his plans for us. Moses' reassurance to fear-ridden Israelites brings courage to our hearts also. "But Moses answered the people, 'Fear not! Stand your ground, and you will see the victory the Lord will win for you today. These Egyptians whom you see today you will never see again. The Lord himself will fight for you; you have only to keep still.' " (Ex 14:13–14)

God would not desert his people. The waters parted, and the Chosen People crossed over on dry land. That same channel became the burial ground of the Egyptian army. God caused the waters to flow back, and they perished.

In his prayer one of my retreatants envisioned Moses happily turning around to thank God for destroying their enemies. When Moses did so, he saw God weeping. When Moses asked God the reason for the tears, God replied: "The Egyptians are also my children."

Our heavenly Father wants to share his creative love with us, expressed in calling us into existence and endowing us with the gift of life. He calls us out of nothingness and gives us zest for enjoying life to the full.

However, our world is wounded by the ravages of sin. Sin scars and cripples us. We have no right to receive the outpouring of God's divine life into our being. We inherited the effects of sinfulness, separating us from God.

Yet love always finds a way. By its very nature love wants to be close to the beloved, to be united with the one loved. Impelled by his boundless love for us, our gracious Father removed the obstacles blocking our way to him.

The Father sent his only begotten Son into the world to redeem us, to reestablish our fractured and fragmented relationship with him. By his Incarnation, Jesus, the all-holy God-Man, assumed our human nature, with all its sinfulness, its brokenness, its physical, psychological, and intellectual limitations, that he might redeem it. By his death and resurrection Jesus reestablished our union with God by sharing his own resurrected life with us.

To continue his redemptive work throughout the yet unborn ages, Jesus founded his healing church. Through the sacramental channel of baptism our union with God is restored and that infinite gap between God and his estranged creatures, between holiness and sinfulness, is spanned.

We are invited to become members of God's family. Our gracious Father adopts us as his sons and daughters: "We are children of God. But if we are children, we are heirs as well: heirs of God, heirs with Christ, if only we suffer with him so as to be glorified with him" (Rom 8:16–17).

As did the Israelites, we, too, cross into our new life of freedom. St. Augustine reminds us: "You, too, left Egypt when, at Baptism, you renounced that world which is at enmity with God."

By virtue of baptism, we become temples of the Holy Spirit abiding with us and within us: "Are you not aware that you are the temple of God, and that the Spirit of God dwells in you? If anyone destroys God's temple, God will destroy him. For the temple of God is holy, and you are that temple." (1 Cor 3:16–17)

This truth is so startling that Paul fears that we may not have comprehended its full significance, so he emphasizes it. "You must know that your body is a temple of the Holy Spirit, who is within — the Spirit you have received from God. You are not your own. You have been purchased, and at a price! So glorify God in your body." (1 Cor 6:19–20)

Again, Paul realizes that our conceptual minds are slow to grasp profound spiritual truths; hence he states again: "You are the temple of the living God, just as God has said: 'I will dwell with them and walk among them. I will be their God and they shall be my people.' " (2 Cor 6:16)

Repetition creates habits within us, which form our attitudes and transform our lifestyle.

We are baptized only once, but baptism is so important in our lives that we need to remind ourselves of its significance. During the Easter vigil and at other appropriate times we relive and reexperience liturgically our baptism, a symbolic drowning of our sinful human nature and an emerging from the font as resurrected persons. It is a tomb and a womb, a grave and a rebirth.

The Israelites crossed the Red Sea only through the interventive power of God. Only through that same power are we able, through baptism, to cross from a state of alienation from God into personal friendship with him.

> The Apostle teaches you that "our fathers were all under the cloud and all passed through the sea; by the cloud and the sea all of them were baptized into Moses" (1 Cor 10:1–2). Further, Moses in his canticle says: "You sent your spirit, and the sea overwhelmed them." You observe that in this crossing by the Hebrews there was already a symbol of holy baptism. The Egyptians perished; the Hebrews escaped. What else is the daily lesson of this sacrament than that guilt is drowned, and error destroyed, while goodness and innocence pass unharmed.
>
> (St. Ambrose on baptism)

By the Exodus, we mean the departure of the Israelites out of the Egyptian slavery into the uncharted way of the desert and eventually to the Promised Land. A whole people venturing into the unknown, called to trust in God. We, too, are part of that Chosen People.

> You, however, are "a chosen race, a royal priesthood, a holy nation, a people he claims as his own to proclaim the glorious works" of the One who called you from darkness into his marvelous light. Once you were no people, but now you are God's people; once there was no mercy for you, but now you have found mercy. (1 Pt 2:9-10)

Our loving Father calls us to be his people. He has plans for each one of us.

> For I know well the plans I have in mind for you, says the Lord, plans for your welfare, not for woe! plans to give you a future full of hope. When you call me, when you go to pray to me, I will listen to you. When you look for me, you will find me. Yes, when you seek me with all your heart, you will find me with you, says the Lord, and I will change your lot. (Jer 29:11-14)

Listening to his Word deepens our awareness of how important, how special we are to our loving Father. Our parents, with our godparents, brought us to the redeeming waters of baptism. At the font we were set apart, freed to become members of the family of God and to discover the plans our Father has for us in this land of sojourn.

Jesus gave us the sacrament of baptism as the starting point in life's pilgrimage, which eventually brings us to the holy mountain of the Lord: "I solemnly assure you, no one can see the reign of God unless he is begotten from above" (Jn 3:3).

He tells us that we must be reborn through the purifying waters of baptism. This rebirth is the work of the Holy Spirit: "I solemnly assure you, no one can enter into God's kingdom without being begotten of water and Spirit" (Jn 3:5).

The power of God's love was manifested at the crossing of the Red Sea. In baptism that same love propels us across the chasm separating us from God into loving union with him. The fruit of that purifying love is eternal bliss with the risen Jesus.

Are you not aware that we who were baptized into Christ Jesus were baptized into his death? Through baptism into his death we were buried with him, so that, just as Christ was raised from the dead by the glory of the Father, we too might live a new life. If we have been united with him through likeness to his death, so shall we be through a like resurrection. (Rom 6:3–5)

We are a privileged people. As we contemplate the magnitude of the personal love of the Father for each one of us, our hearts yearn to respond to him with all the love and gratitude we can muster.

TWO

Desert Silence

Come to me heedfully, listen, that you may have life.
(Is 55:3)

I will lead her into the desert and speak to her heart.
(Hos 2:16)

BAPTISM IS ESSENTIAL but it is only the first step on our journey heavenward. It initiates us into God's plan of salvation. A conditioning process follows. Athletes submit to rigorous training programs in conditioning themselves physically and mentally to enter a contest. Our journey to our eternal union with our loving Father requires spiritual conditioning.

After the Israelites had safely and miraculously crossed the Red Sea, they found themselves in the desert. The desert, too, is God's special abode. God is omnipresent, but we can more easily discover him in the vast emptiness and bleak barrenness of the desert. Its very bleakness helps us to rise above the many demands and distractions of daily living and enables us to rivet our focus on God who becomes more real to us in solitude. In the desert or on a mountain we can more easily become aware of God's mysterious presence.

God guided his people into the desert that there they could recognize him as Lord and God. Their mentality and relationship to him as Creator and Lord had to be formed. There they were brought to realize their dependence on him. Their very existence depended upon his providential love for them.

The Israelites were on their way to Mount Sinai, where God wanted to make them a covenanted people, but first they had to learn who they were and who God is. This was the starting point in their relationship with him.

We too must find our way to Mount Sinai to meet our Father. In our desert experience a personal relationship with our Father is formed, correct priorities established.

Some time ago, while visiting a family, I discovered a stack of sleeping bags in the living room. Observing my surprise the father explained that they were mountain climbers, soon to launch upon another expedition. They were sleeping on the floor to condition themselves for sleeping on the rough terrain of the mountains.

The next morning we walked together for several miles. This was also part of the conditioning process. After weeks of such training they were more prepared for their next climb.

We too need conditioning. With the Israelites we travel into the desert. All we see is sand and more sand, rocks and more rocks — seemingly endless miles of emptiness. We feel lost, alone, bewildered, weak, and unable to journey farther. Walking is difficult over rocks and shifting sands. Our feet are scorched; wind-blown sand obscures our vision like storm clouds, causing us to lose our sense of direction. The emptiness, solitude, and stillness of the desert make us aware of the presence of God. Its vastness reminds us of his immensity.

There we become more poignantly aware of our need for God. We are totally dependent upon him even for very survival. We are helpless. We have no food, no drink. There is not a green leaf to be seen, nor a blade of grass, not even a dry stem. We are famished, but there is no food. No fruit trees, no berries, no roots to stave off gnawing hunger pangs. Our throats become parched, but there is no water to relieve distress and pain.

In the desert God stripped the Israelites of everything so that they could experience their own helplessness, their complete dependence upon him. When the Israelites first experienced their dire need, they rebelled.

Here in the desert the whole Israelite community grumbled against Moses and Aaron. The Israelites said to them, "Would that we had died at the Lord's hand in the land of Egypt, as we sat by our flesh pots and ate our fill of bread! But you had to lead us into this desert to make the whole community die of famine!" (Ex 16:2–3)

Are our own attitudes similar to that of the transient Israelites? Do we question God's ways in our own lives, perhaps even rebel?

In spite of our rebellion God responds to our needs with the same patience and graciousness he showed the Israelites:

Then the Lord said to Moses, "I will now rain down bread from heaven for you. Each day the people are to go out and gather their daily portion; thus will I test them, to see whether they follow my instructions or not." (Ex 16:4)

And when they continued to grumble:

The Lord spoke to Moses and said, "I have heard the grumbling of the Israelites. Tell them: In the evening twilight you shall eat flesh, and in the morning you shall have your fill of bread, so that you may know that I, the Lord, am your God."

(Ex 16:11–12)

In his providential love God was faithful to his promise: "In the evening quail came up and covered the camp" (Ex 16:13).

God supplied them with water by directing Moses to strike the rock with the same staff with which he struck the waters of the Red Sea.

As the Israelites experienced helplessness they developed poverty of spirit—a growing awareness of their own inadequacy and their total dependence upon God. This expanded consciousness would never have developed without their desert experience.

I have spoken glibly for years about God stripping the Chosen People of everything in the desert in order to bring them to an awareness of their dependence upon him. However, only when I was privileged to travel through the Sinai Desert with its terrible rocky beauty and its emptiness was I able to understand that total dependence upon an all-good God for survival.

In the desert of life, we become more aware of our own helplessness to survive, our total dependence upon the providence of our caring Father. "Your heavenly Father knows all that you need. Seek first his kingship over you, his way of holiness, and all these things will be given you besides." (Mt 6:32–33)

What is God asking of us? How can we better seek and find him than in the solitude of a desert? How much we take for granted! How seldom we realize that "every worthwhile gift, every genuine benefit comes from above, descending from the Father of the heavenly luminaries, who cannot change and who is never shadowed over" (Jas 1:17).

Every heartbeat is a gift from our creating Father. His providing love envelopes our whole life. It is easy to take it all for granted and fail to thank him.

Our loving Father provides for every physical need and also wants us to be happy, to experience his peace and joy. Jesus came to bring us the Good News of our redemption and resurrection so that we could be a joyous people: "All this I tell you that my joy may be yours and your joy may be complete" (Jn 15:11).

He invites us to know him better, by listening to him with our whole being. He invites us to journey into the desert that we may eventually come into his presence on our own Mount Sinai.

We need a desert experience to rest and relax in the loving arms of our Father. We need to pause, to reflect, to ponder, and to take inventory of all that our Father is doing for us. We need to ascertain who we are and who God is.

The desert affects us mightily and brings us into a deeper awareness of the presence and power of God. We may not be able to find a geographic desert away from the noise, speed, and confusion of modern society, but there are a variety of deserts available.

Spending time listening to the Lord each day is a valuable desert experience. The transcendent God of heaven and earth wants to communicate with us, his creatures. This is not the blaring communication of the world. It requires the silence and solitude which only a desert can provide.

Daily visits with our loving Father create and solidify a deep, personal relationship unattainable by other means. We come to know him as a gracious, loving Father who cares for us at every moment of the day. The Lord pleads: "Be still and know that I am God" (Ps 46:11, Grail translation). And again, "Be still before the Lord and wait in patience" (Ps 37:7, Grail translation).

Where can we find such a desert? Our own home is the best oratory. A prayer room or den with a prayer shelf, our favorite chair, our bedroom — any of these can be a hallowed spot where we meet the Lord each day. These daily periods with him lift our vision and give purpose to our whole day. They orient our life Godward.

At times Jesus invites us to spend a longer, more formal time with him in prayer. When the disciples returned from their mission of healing and preaching the Good News, Jesus invited them to come apart in order to reflect on what God was doing in them and through them for others. "People were coming and going in great numbers" (Mk 6:31). Jesus knew that in the midst of this hubbub the disciples could not understand the power of God working in them. It was then that he invited his disciples, "Come by yourselves to an out-of-the-way place and rest a little" (Mk 6:31).

Jesus invites us to do the same — to make a day of prayer, recollection, or renewal at a retreat center, a hermitage, a house of prayer, or even in our own home.

A friend of mine set up a prayer room in her home. When her daughter married she converted the extra bedroom into a poustinia room, often used by friends who also want time alone with the Lord.

We may be able to spend a whole day with the Lord, or perhaps only a few hours. Whatever we are able to give the Lord is graciously accepted by him and fruitful in our spiritual journey.

The Lord may ask us to spend a longer sojourn with him in a contemplative retreat. This is a time of listening under the guidance of a spiritual director, enabling us to discern the Lord's loving plan for us. It is a valuable time away from the hurried, rushed atmosphere of jangling telephones, tantalizing television, and blaring radio — a time to withdraw from the tensions and turmoil of everyday living to keep our focus riveted on the Lord and our final destiny. It is a precious time of inspiration, motivation, and transformation, an ideal desert experience.

There are many demands in daily routine. We may feel there

just isn't enough time for prayer or for a retreat. When such a temptation assails us, listen to Jesus' reproach to his disciples: "So you could not stay awake with me for even an hour?" (Mt 26:40).

Jesus leads us into the desert by his own example. Before beginning his mission of preaching the Good News, "Jesus was led into the desert by the Spirit to be tempted by the devil" (Mt 4:1). And after an ordeal of healing and driving out demons, "rising early the next morning, he went off to a lonely place in the desert; there he was absorbed in prayer" (Mk 1:35).

Jesus also found a mountain retreat conducive to prayer. Before selecting his apostles, "he went out to the mountain to pray, spending the night in communion with God" (Lk 6:12).

And before ending his ministry in suffering, Jesus sought strength and support in prayer, again on a mountaintop. Laconically the evangelist says: "He took Peter, John and James, and went up onto a mountain to pray" (Lk 9:28). After Jesus had spent time in prayer he accepted fully the Father's will. It was then that the Taboric splendor radiated from him to the disciples.

Jesus shows us the need for prayer and conditioning for our ministry. John the Baptist, too, spent much time in the desert, preparing himself for his mission as "a herald's voice in the desert" (Lk 3:4).

Paul, after his conversion on the road to Damascus, felt called into the desert where the Lord transformed and equipped him to bring the Good News to the Gentile world (Gal 1:17).

The desert is a place for listening. We need silence and solitude, peace and quiet to be able to listen to God well. This is why the Lord leads us into the desert.

Listening is not easy. It is an art. Noises bombard us, and we have learned to turn off certain things in our daily living. We do so for our own well-being, since these jangling noises threaten our peace of mind.

Listening is more than just hearing. Listening is putting ourselves totally at the disposal of others. We forget self.

Listening is actively being silent with another person. It is silently being for another person. We can be silent, but not listening. We can be silently alone with our own thoughts, but not be open and receptive to what the Lord is trying to communicate to us.

Listening is participating in another's life in a creative and powerful way. A listener is quiet and sensitive toward another person, open and active, receptive and alive.

This kind of listening is an art which the Lord will teach us in the desert of our own hearts. Listening to God with our whole being means "being" for God and letting him "be" for us. Listening is putting ourselves totally at his disposal. It is prayer at its best.

Listening is vital to our relationship with our loving Father, because we cannot love a person we do not know, nor can we know a person to whom we have not listened. Love is at the heart of our spiritual journey.

Proper listening is never artificial or stilted. It is warm, interested, concerned. Listening is love in action. Listening to God is prayer. It is hearing the Spirit of God, who dwells in our hearts, speaking to us. Real listening is experiencing God. It is God communing with us.

In the *Summa Theologica*, St. Thomas Aquinas accomplished a monumental task, giving reason and rationale for revealed truth. After experiencing God contemplatively and giving us such a masterpiece of systematized theology, he is said to have instructed his secretary to burn everything he had written, for he considered it but straw compared to his experiential knowledge of God.

This kind of knowledge of God comes only from listening. When we listen on this level we touch the deepest levels where the Spirit of the living Jesus draws us into deeper union with him. Such listening helps us discover what is of God and what is not. It enables us to understand better that we are the temples of the Holy Spirit. It occasions a rich communion with God.

Furthermore, listening in this fashion helps us arrive at the true worth of another person. God is present in every human being, and listening puts us in touch with that presence. Listening in the Spirit brings us to love others with a divine love. It inspires reverence for God's creation and our union with others in the Body of Christ. When we know this oneness, we know a holy secret.

It is surprising how often the word "listen" and its synonyms are used in Scripture. God does nothing in vain. He is asking us to listen because it is so important for our spiritual growth.

"Come to me heedfully, listen, that you may have life!" (Is 55:3).

How pleased our Father is when we respond as did young Samuel: "Speak, Lord, for your servant is listening" (1 Sm 3:9).

The Father, on Mount Tabor, urges, "This is my Son, my Chosen One. Listen to him." (Lk 9:35).

In the desert of our own hearts, we listen to what our Father says, and he is pleased.

In listening we know him as a gracious, loving Abba; but more importantly, we know that we are precious to him and that he loves us just as we are.

When we pray well we listen with our whole being; we become aware of the Lord's presence. We experience him with us and within us. At times he seems outside us or even far away from us. We may feel his love enveloping us like the warm rays of the sun, or we may be left to find him in silence or in dryness and distraction. We may feel his presence as joy or as fullness, but if we expect him in joy he may come in sorrow. We may give up waiting for him, and yet find him waiting for us. God is a God of surprises.

The desert teaches us much about our relationship to the Father. Paradoxically, we must first experience our nothingness to discover our true worth. We must recognize our emptiness, so that he can fill us with himself.

A desert experience is a powerful means of conditioning us in our pilgrimage to our loving Father.

THREE

Mount of Compassion and Covenant

Come, let us climb the Lord's mountain...that he may instruct us in his ways, and we may walk in his paths.

(Is 2:3)

OUR PURPOSE IN LIFE is to grow in our personal relationship with God, to know him as a personal God, a loving, caring Father, a gracious God who gifts us not only with life but provides for our every human need — the air we breathe, the food we eat, the water which quenches our thirst. He himself assures us that he loves us with an enduring love: "You are precious in my eyes, and glorious and...I love you" (Is 43:4). Again, "With an age-old love I have loved you; so I have kept my mercy toward you" (Jer 31:3).

We cannot love a person whom we do not know, and we cannot know a person to whom we have not listened. In prayer we are invited to listen to God. He speaks to our hearts of his love for us, his acceptance of us just as we are. This truth is exemplified in the history of the Chosen People. We journey with the Israelites and learn from their experience.

Survival in the desert was impossible with natural resources only. Their generous God provided them with manna or heaven-bread, with meat of quail, and with abundant water from a rock. Their faith in this God who was concerned for them was beginning to develop. Then, after their wanderings in the desert, where they recognized their need of God and dependence on him, God brought them to Mount Sinai where he wanted to form them into his people: "You shall be my people, and I will be your God" (Jer 30:22). Through his prophet, our loving Father invites us as well, "Come, let us climb the Lord's mountain...that he may instruct us in his ways, and we may walk in his paths" (Is 2:3).

We stand in awe at the majestic sight of a towering mountain. The sheer immensity of a mountain speaks to us of the power and presence of the Lord. "In his hands are the depths of the earth, and the tops of the mountains are his" (Ps 95:4). Though figurative language, it is an apt image for God's mysterious presence among us.

The Israelites experienced God in a unique way on Mount Sinai: "The glory of the Lord settled upon Mount Sinai.... To the Israelites the glory of the Lord was seen as a consuming fire on the mountaintop." (Ex 24:16–17)

Chosen People

This encounter with God on Mount Sinai was a tremendous experience for the Israelites. On its height God revealed his glory and power. He set forth a code of law which established a personal relationship with him and taught the Israelites to live in peace and harmony with each other.

According to the culture of that day a group of people without a code of law was considered little more than a band of fugitives. Once they were bound by a code of law, they became a nation, a people.

Until this time the Israelites were a motley crowd of runaway slaves. Then God called them to Mount Sinai, gave them a law, and formed them into a nation—his Chosen People. They were now to be reckoned with.

God also revealed much about himself on Mount Sinai:

I, the Lord, am your God.... You shall not have other gods besides me.... For I, the Lord, your God, am a jealous God... bestowing mercy, down to the thousandth generation, on the children of those who love me and keep my commandments.

(Dt 5:6–7, 9)

As a loving Father, God does not force us to accept his will. He respects the freedom with which he endowed us. His commandments forbid license but give us true liberty. For example, the Fifth Commandment, by forbidding us to take the life of another person, protects our own right to life.

God was speaking to all and for all times and to us when he said, "I have set before you life and death, the blessing and the curse. Choose life, then, that you and your descendants may live, by loving the Lord, your God, heeding his voice, and holding fast to him." (Dt 30:19–20)

God challenged his people to live according to "his commandments, statutes and decrees." He spoke to his people through Moses, who spoke "face to face" with God. Moses in turn related God's message to the people. "When Moses came to the people and related all the words and ordinances of the Lord, they all answered with one voice, 'We will do everything that the Lord has told us' " (Ex 24:3).

Moses wanted the people to understand thoroughly what God was asking of them. He wanted them to comprehend the commitment they were about to make. This was a necessary condition before the covenant could be solemnly ratified. Therefore, "rising early the next day, he erected at the foot of the mountain an altar.... Taking the book of the covenant, he read it aloud to the people, who answered, 'All that the Lord has said, we will heed and do.' " (Ex 24:4, 7)

After the ratification of the covenant Moses went back up Mount Sinai. "After Moses had gone up, a cloud covered the mountain. The glory of the Lord settled upon Mount Sinai.... To the Israelites the glory of the Lord was seen as a consuming fire on the mountaintop." (Ex 24:15–17)

God manifested his presence to show his pleasure at their commitment to his covenant. They accepted him as a loving Father, guiding them on their pilgrimage through life.

The Golden Calf

The fidelity of the Chosen People was short-lived. They soon tired of the covenant they had made with the Lord. In their human frailty they longed for the fleshpots of Egypt. The God they had met so recently was too intangible, too spiritual, too transcendent. Their pragmatic minds wanted a god they could see and one they could worship with a ritual of their own. Before long they reverted to the pagan gods of Egypt.

While Moses was communing with God on the mountaintop, the Israelites below came to Aaron, begging him to cast them a god and contributing their jewelry for the project. Soon a golden calf was fashioned for them, an altar was built, and they were deeply engrossed in their idolatrous worship, bringing peace oblations and offering holocausts to their golden calf god.

How quickly they turned from their gracious God who had miraculously rescued them from the slavery of Egypt. They were blinded to the outpouring of his love, even as he was sustaining them with bread, meat, and water. They were momentarily oblivious of the fact that their feet never grew weary or sore and that their clothes did not wear out.

Their complete absorption in this idol blinded them. They preferred a golden calf to a loving, gracious, personal Father. The pagan customs and influences of Egypt were still deeply ingrained in them.

Moses had told them, "You shall not worship any other god, for the Lord is 'the Jealous One'; a jealous God is he" (Ex 34:14).

God is not jealous for personal gain. He knew that worship of any false deity could never bring peace and happiness to the Israelites. God wanted to spare them this disappointment; hence he claimed their worship exclusively for himself.

Moses censored them: "You have commited a grave sin" (Ex 32:30). God was disappointed and angry with his Chosen People: "Let me alone, then, that my wrath may blaze up against them to consume them" (Ex 32:10). But Moses interceded:

"Let your blazing wrath die down; relent in punishing your people.". . . So Moses went back to the Lord and said: "Ah, this people has indeed committed a grave sin in making a god of gold for themselves! If you would only forgive their sin!"
(Ex 32:12, 30)

In prayer we climb the mountain of the Lord. God meets us there. In prayer we experience the unique presence of the Lord. We discover in a deeper way his providential care and loving concern for us.

In more generous moments we may have commited ourselves to his will regardless of what he might ask or where he may lead. Unfortunately, for us, as for the Israelites, many false gods begin to appear along our earthly journey.

The god of self-centeredness and self-sufficiency raises its enticing head, and it is easy to succomb to its wiles, to rationalize that we must first take care of ourselves.

The god of pride often trips us up on the path to the mountain of the Lord, easily hurt and wounded, offended if someone else is honored or preferred to us. Pride causes us to judge others, even though Jesus advises us, "Be compassionate, as your Father is compassionate. Do not judge, and you will not be judged. Do not condemn, and you will not be condemned. Pardon, and you shall be pardoned." (Lk 6:36-37)

We can readily agree with Jesus' advice, but when threatened we can react quickly and forget easily. Through Jeremiah God reminds us, "I, the Lord, alone probe the mind and test the heart, reward everyone according to his ways, according to the merit of his deeds" (Jer 17:10).

The golden calf, ever present in our lives, may be a long list of secular standards. When unduly concerned about what others may think, insecurity challenges us to prove ourselves, so we strive for a better education and a higher standard of living than our neighbors'.

Power, reputation, social standing, inordinate desires for a new car, a bigger house, a world tour to improve our social standing — all these may be golden calves for us, requiring all our attention and energy.

At Sinai God manifested himself as a merciful, compassionate, forgiving God. His healing love prevailed. He forgave his people. He took them back. As he expressed later through Hosea, "How could I give you up, O Ephraim, or deliver you up, O Israel?" (Hos 11:8). He continued to lead the Israelites through the desert with a pillar of cloud by day and a column of fire by night, until they reached the Promised Land.

God our Father's love never changes. He continues to pour out his forgiveness simply because he loves us. "It is I, I, who wipe out for my own sake, your offenses; your sins I remember no more" (Is 43:25).

Jesus assures us that he, too, is merciful and forgiving. His forgiveness in the sacrament of reconciliation is personal. He assures us there: "Your sins are forgiven you." Gracious was his promise to the good thief on the cross: "I assure you: this day you will be with me in paradise" (Lk 23:43).

The few conditions he places on this loving forgiveness are minimal: he asks us to be open and receptive to his will and to permit him to fill us with his "living waters," washing away all our sinfulness. He wants us to be ever mindful that he loves us just as we are, regardless of what we may have done.

In other words, God must come first in our life. "For I, the Lord, your God, am a jealous God" (Ex 20:5). Our focus must always be on him as our final goal. Every decision must be made in the light of our friendship with him. Our chief concern must always be: "What would God want me to do in this situation?"

Jesus was always attuned to the will of his Father. His principal concern was to do the will of his Father, regardless of the cost — and it cost him his life. "It is not to do my own will that I have come down from heaven, but to do the will of him who sent me" (Jn 6:38).

How Can We Know God's Will?

"What does God want me to do here and now?"

As we come to know people better, our love for them grows and matures. We become sensitized to their likes and dislikes. We begin to know what pleases them and what causes annoyance. We can often anticipate their wishes.

The same is true of our Father in heaven. As we grow to know him better we sense what he wishes. As our will becomes more attuned to his we better discern his will.

One fruit of knowing and doing his will is the peace which fills our hearts. When thoughts and conduct are in harmony with God's will, there is much peace.

Our loving Father invites us to climb Mount Sinai once again. He wants to meet us and wants us to know him better.

As we rest and relax in his presence on the top of the mountain we comprehend that his laws are not meant just to curb and control us, not mere whims of a God who wants to take advantage of us. His laws place restrictions only on license, but give real liberty. Each law has a very positive dimension. If I may not steal from my neighbor, nor take his life at will, my life and property and rights must be respected.

Basking in the sunshine of God's presence on the mountaintop, we are taught that he loves us, that he wants our happiness. His commandments are directives to assure it. As Jesus promised, "Anyone who loves me will be true to my word, and my Father will love him; we will come to him and make our dwelling place with him" (Jn 14:23).

At Sinai we meet our loving, creating, providing Father who guides us to our eternal destiny. "You shall be my people, and I will be your God" (Jer 30:22).

FOUR

Mount of Decision

He is to be your God and you are to walk in his ways.
(Dt 26:17)

AFTER THE ISRAELITES had wandered through the desert for forty years, they came into the vicinity of Mount Nebo in the land of Moab over against the city of Jericho. Here God said to Moses, "Go up here into the Abarim Mountains and view the land that I am giving to the Israelites" (Nm 27:12).

Mount Nebo is 2,645 feet above sea level and has a commanding view of the surrounding terrain, especially to the west. From this point Moses surveyed the whole Promised Land. However, to reach it the Israelites had to cross the Jordan River. This crossing was to be carried out according to the plan God had outlined and in the manner he had prescribed.

In spirit we left Mount Sinai with the Chosen People, where we came to know God, not only as a God of might and power, but as a loving Father who provides for us and protects us at every moment of the day. On our spiritual pilgrimage we continue through the Negeb Desert and on to Mount Nebo.

From Mount Nebo we can view the Promised Land, the land of the Holy One, where Jesus spent his earthly sojourn. In this land he announced that the reign of God was at hand; he proclaimed the Good News and worked his many miracles; he healed the sick, the lame, and the blind; he taught continually, laying down the conditions for becoming one of his followers; he manifested his power over life and death by restoring life to some persons who had died. All of this flashes before our minds as in spirit we stand on the top of Mount Nebo surveying the Promised Land.

As Paul in a vision saw a man of Macedonia inviting him to come over to Macedonia (Acts 16:9), Jesus invites us to cross the Jordan and come with him into the Promised Land. His reassuring invitation is this:

> Come to me, all you who are weary and find life burdensome, and I will refresh you. Take my yoke upon your shoulders and learn from me, for I am gentle and humble of heart. Your souls will find rest, for my yoke is easy and my burden light.
>
> (Mt 11:28–30)

We cannot assume our role as disciples of Jesus without being called by him. Both the call and the courage to respond must come from him. "It was not you who chose me, it was I who chose you to go forth and bear fruit. Your fruit must endure, so that all you ask the Father in my name he will give you." (Jn 15:16) "Come follow me." He challenges us to dare to love as unselfishly as he loved. The decision is ours. Will we, or will we not, cross the Jordan?

Jesus does not trick us into deciding to become his disciples. The conditions are clearly spelled out: "Unless the grain of wheat falls to the earth and dies, it remains just a grain of wheat. But if it dies, it produces much fruit." (Jn 12:24)

And the dispositions necessary for becoming his disciples?

> Whoever wishes to be my follower must deny his very self, take up his cross each day, and follow in my steps. (Lk 9:23)

> Whoever would save his life will lose it, but whoever loses his life for my sake will find it. What profit would a man show if he were to gain the whole world and destroy himself in the process? (Mt 16:24–25)

What is required to follow Jesus? Everything. Halfway measures will not suffice. Love must give all.

To a would-be follower Jesus replies, "Let the dead bury their dead" (Lk 9:60). This prospective disciple wanted to remain home until his father had died. When he had no other family ties, then he would be willing to follow Jesus. Jesus was saying that the other relatives still at home would take care of the father.

To another potential disciple: "Whoever puts his hand to the plow but keeps looking back is unfit for the reign of God" (Lk 9:62). His hearers understood how impossible it is to plow a straight furrow if one keeps looking back. A would-be follower cannot give himself totally to Jesus unless he is willing to cross that symbolic river and make a firm commitment never to turn back.

At times we might have to sever some family ties in order to dedicate ourselves totally to his call to discipleship. "If anyone comes to me without turning his back on his father and mother, his wife and his children, his brothers and sisters, indeed his very self, he cannot be my follower" (Lk 14:25–26).

The cost of discipleship may initially seem very high. However, as we ponder the privilege and the reward of discipleship we realize the cost is relatively small.

The indispensable requisite for choosing to cross the Jordan and follow Jesus is love. When we experience the infinite love that Jesus has for us, we can respond in love to become a dedicated disciple without counting the cost.

In the outpouring of the love of Jesus for us, our response minimizes the cost of discipleship. Jesus' love for us is infinite and immutable. "As the Father has loved me, so I have loved you. Live in my love." (Jn 15:9) We live on in his love when we strive to live his way of life and fulfill all he asks of us. "You will live in my love if you keep my commandments" (Jn 15:10).

As we stand in spirit on Mount Nebo, gazing into the Promised Land and weighing the conditions for entering a close, personal relationship with Jesus, all heaven seems to wait on our choice.

Our purpose is to follow Jesus and put on his image. We cannot form a deep love relationship with him unless we know him. And to know him we must spend time with him, listening to him. This prayer will transform us so that we can be identified with Jesus. Jesus invites us to "come and see," to cross the Jordan River, accepting his invitation to be his disciple. He asks us to journey with him, listening to the Word he proclaims, learning from him as he reaches out in love to all who come to him, resting in his presence, opening our hearts to his love.

To accept the divine invitation, we must figuratively cross the Jordan. Crossing the River Jordan symbolizes our resolve to follow Jesus and become his disciples. The decision to cross the Jordan is not our final commitment. Our sojourn is ongoing.

Before the Israelites were permitted to cross into the Promised Land, they received specific instructions from God about how they were to proceed. The central concern was the ark of the covenant, which represented the presence of God in their midst. God wanted to manifest his power.

> The ark of the covenant of the Lord of the whole earth will precede you into the Jordan.... When the soles of the feet of priests carrying the ark of the Lord, the Lord of the whole earth, touch the water of the Jordan, it will cease to flow; for the water flowing down from upstream will halt in a solid bank.
>
> (Jos 3:11, 13)

God wanted his people to know who was guiding and directing them and that without him they could do nothing. This episode speaks eloquently to us of our own inadequacy and dependency. We cannot succeed in following Jesus without God's help. "No one can come to me unless the Father who sent me draws him" (Jn 6:44). Again, "Apart from me you can do nothing" (Jn 15:5).

Only after the disciples admitted their helplessness did Jesus feed the multitude with "five barley loaves and a couple of dried fish" (Jn 6:1-13). On other occasions as well, it was after the apostles acknowledged their inability that Jesus took over.

The decision to accept and live the lifestyle of Jesus requires grace from God our loving Father. Adequate divine help will be there if we ask for it and are open to receive it.

To be receptive to God's help requires detaching ourselves from the persons, places, and things preventing us from giving our unconditional assent to the Lord. It means a "letting go" and "letting God." There may be misgivings, fear that God may ask too much of us—more than we wish to give, or more than we think we are able to give. We may hesitate to give without reservation whatever he asks of us, not knowing where he may lead us.

Christian life consists in dying to self and thus giving ourselves more to the Lord so that he may fill us with himself. Dying to self-centeredness is sometimes difficult until we experience the joy of giving ourselves in love to God. Each day dying to self means a greater capacity to receive the influx of God's divine life and love.

There can be many roadblocks along life's highway, and we may not even be aware of them. However, in the sunshine of God's presence these hindrances become more apparent. With God's help, we can remove or overcome them.

The injunction God gave to the Israelites before they crossed the River Jordan also applies to all the attachments which would deflect our attention from the Lord.

If you do not drive out the inhabitants of the land before you, those whom you allow to remain will become as barbs in your eyes and thorns in your sides, and they will harass you in the country where you live, and I will treat you as I had intended to treat them. (Nm 33:55–56)

Our self-will, our attachments, our self-centeredness can easily become "barbs in our eyes and thorns in our sides" as we cross the Jordan by choosing to become his disciples. Part of the conditioning process is recognizing these barbs and thorns and permitting Jesus to prune us so that we may bear even more fruit.

When we choose to follow Jesus and to implement our commitment by crossing the Jordan into his homeland, the Father is very much pleased. He wants to make a covenant with us as he did with the Chosen People.

Today you are making this agreement with the Lord: he is to be your God and you are to walk in his ways and observe his statutes, commandments and decrees and to harken to his voice. And today the Lord is making this agreement with you: you are to be a people peculiarly his own, as he promised you; and provided you keep his commandments, he will then raise you high in praise and renown and glory above all other nations he has made, and you will be a people sacred to the Lord, your God, as he promised. (Dt 26:17–19)

When we cross our Jordan, we do become "a people peculiarly his own." In baptism we were incorporated into the Body of his Son. We became the people of God—his adopted sons and daughters: "You are the temple of the living God, just as God has said: 'I will dwell with them and walk among them. I will be their God and they shall be my people.' " (2 Cor 6:16)

After our baptism Jesus asks for a deeper commitment; he asks us to make the psalmist's words our own: "To do your will, O God, is my delight, and your law is within my heart" (Ps 40:9).

Furthermore, by committing our lives more totally to Jesus we become his friends. "You are my friends if you do what I command you" (Jn 15:14).

No greater companion and friend could we have than Jesus as we journey through life! And he himself assures us, "Know that I am with you always, until the end of the world" (Mt 28:20).

FIVE

His Way of Life

Blest are they who hear the word of God and keep it.
(Lk 11:28)

AFTER WE DECIDE to follow Jesus and to commit ourselves to being his disciples, we are ready to cross the Jordan River into a new way of life. Jesus beckons us toward the Mount of Beatitudes.

We climb its gentle slope to come closer to Jesus and listen to his words. Jesus is pleased to share the Good News with us. "When he saw the crowds he went up on the mountainside. After he had sat down his disciples gathered around him, and he began to teach them." (Mt 5:1–2).

In the spring the slopes of the Mount of Beatitudes are a bit of heaven covering the earth. The whole Mount and the plain below are carpeted with gorgeous wild flowers of every shade and hue. Crimson anemones seem to dominate.

The beauty of God's creative handiwork is a delight. We stand in awe trying to absorb it all. Then Jesus says, "Learn a lesson from the way the wild flowers grow. They do not work, they do not spin. Yet I assure you, not even Solomon in all his splendor was arrayed like one of these." (Mt 6:28–29) Flocks of birds sing and praise the provident God who takes such tender care of them. Jesus is aware of them also. "Look at the birds in the sky. They do not sow or reap, they gather nothing into barns; yet your heavenly Father feeds them." (Mt 6:26) And then his all-important question, "Are not you more important than they?" (Mt 6:26).

This awareness of the Father's providential love for us brings much peace. If our beneficent Father is providing for our every need, there is no place for worry or anxiety in our lives. "Seek first his kingship over you, his way of holiness, and all these things will be given you besides" (Mt 6:33).

The words of Jesus touch us deeply, and we are mysteriously drawn to him, to hear more, to absorb every utterance which comes from him. We long to close our eyes and be alone in silent contemplation.

In his discourse on the Beatitudes, St. Leo the Great writes: "And so it was that he who had spoken to Moses spoke also to the apostles. . . . And this was not done as formerly, in the midst of dense clouds, amid terrifying sounds and lightning, so that the people were frightened away from approaching the mountain. Instead here was a tranquil discourse so that the harshness of the law might be softened by the gentleness of grace, and the spirit of adoption might dispel the terror of slavery."

Jesus' teaching on the Mount did not abrogate the Decalogue of Mount Sinai, but offered directives and guidelines for a more total commitment as his disciples.

Invitation

When two disciples of John the Baptizer were curious about Jesus he invited them to "come and see" (Jn 1:39). In the same way Jesus invites us to come to him, to abide with him, to learn from him. "Learn from me, for I am gentle and humble of heart" (Mt 11:29). Jesus continues to lead and guide us into his way of life. After he invites us to come to him, he asks us to become his followers, his disciples. "Come and follow me" (Mk 10:21).

A disciple is a person who follows his master so closely that he can eventually be identified with him. A disciple is more than a student or pupil. He does more than just listen to the teachings of the master. A disciple follows the master, learns by listening to him, living with him, observing him under all circumstances. He carefully notes how his master responds to other people and how he reacts in various situations. He strives to capture the mentality, the attitudes, the feelings, the heart of the master. This is how Jesus wants us to become his disciples. This is what he means when he bids us: "Learn from me, for I am gentle and humble of heart."

We are invited to become followers of Jesus. He wants us to listen to him, to imitate him, to take on his mind and heart, and to reflect his attitudes. We cannot do so unless we know him. It is not enough to know *about* Jesus; we must know *him* as a Person. We must know him with an appreciative knowledge, a heart knowledge.

Jesus reveals much about himself in that long discourse on the Mount of Beatitudes, which we often refer to as the Sermon on the Mount.

Self-Revelation

Nowhere in the Gospels do we find a word-picture of the physical appearance of Jesus. We do not know if he was tall or short, light-complexioned or swarthy, thin or stocky. Nor do those pre-camera days furnish us with a photograph or even a pen sketch of Jesus. Yet, while we don't have a description of his physical appearance, we do know something of his personality. In the Beatitudes, he was really giving us a picture of himself. He was revealing his own heart and mind.

His disciples must imitate him closely enough to be identified with him. To do so requires knowing him and all that he represents. In the Beatitudes, Jesus was really saying: "These are the ideals and the qualities I possess; blessed will you be if you are like me in this regard." In effect he was saying, "I am poor in spirit and blessed will you be if you are poor in spirit."

Jesus' lifestyle certainly verified his claim to poverty of spirit. He was so materially poor that he could say to a would-be follower: "The foxes have lairs, the birds of the sky have nests, but the Son of Man has nowhere to lay his head" (Lk 9:58). Jesus was also poor in spirit, for he was totally and completely submissive to his Father's will.

Jesus exemplified the blessedness of "sorrowing." He wept over the fate of Jerusalem because of its lack of faith. He foresaw the destruction which would come to the Holy City because it rejected him.

Weeping with or for someone else, then, is sorrowing as Jesus did.

Jesus is "lowly." The dire poverty of Bethlehem (as well as Nazareth) speaks to us of his lowliness in the eyes of the world. He was low-born, not of the priestly caste or a scholar from rabbinical schools.

Lowliness consists primarily in humility of heart. Recognizing total dependence upon the Lord is an expression of lowliness. A disregard for the standards of the world also speaks of lowliness.

Surely Jesus did "hunger and thirst for holiness." He was holiness personified. "Can any one of you convict me of sin?" (Jn 8:46).

Growing in holiness means striving to fulfill God's commands. This means a frequent dying to self and saying yes to God. It means focusing on the Lord and letting him lead us. "Send forth your light and your fidelity; they shall lead me on and bring me to your holy mountain, to your dwelling place" (Ps 43:3).

As for the loving compassion of Jesus, did he not always and everywhere "show mercy"? "There is no greater love than this: to lay down one's life for one's friends" (Jn 15:13). Jesus translated that love into action the very next day when he did lay down his life for us. He willingly chose to do this for us because he loves us. "I lay down my life to take it up again. No one takes it from me; I lay it down freely" (Jn 10:17).

Jesus revealed his compassion when he prayed for his executioners from his cross: "Father, forgive them; they do not know what they are doing" (Lk 23:34).

Jesus taught, "Blest are the single-hearted." No one was more single-hearted than he was. His sole preoccupation was doing the Father's will at all times. He came to establish his kingdom on earth as his Father desired. At no time in his life did self-concern or self-pity creep into his words or heart.

Single-heartedness gives direction and purpose to life. It brings peace and joy.

Certainly Jesus was a "peacemaker." By his death and resurrection he reestablished peace in our relationship with his Father and with one another. He greeted his apostles after his resurrection with "Peace be with you" (Jn 20:19).

In his farewell address Jesus promised, " 'Peace' is my farewell to you, my peace is my gift to you; I do not give it to you as the world gives peace. Do not be distressed or fearful." (Jn 14:27) Walking in his footsteps affords many occasions to bring peace to others. Peacemakers are singularly blessed.

Jesus was rejected and persecuted from the first moments of his life. The Gospels record continual rejection throughout his sojourn on earth. In addition, Jesus took on the physical, psychological, intellectual limitations of our human nature: "He emptied himself and took the form of a slave, being born in the likeness of men" (Phil 2:7).

The Beatitudes reveal Jesus' personality. He is poor in spirit, lowly, compassionate, and merciful. He is holiness personified, a man of sorrows, single-hearted in doing the Father's will. Even though he is the Prince of Peace, he is rejected and persecuted.

When these Beatitudes become the rule of life, when daily living manifests the spirit which they exemplify, this is putting on the mind of Christ. This is to "put on that new man created in God's image" (Eph 4:24). Those who do are true disciples.

School of Christian Formation

The Mount of Beatitudes, with its commanding view of the Sea of Galilee and its backdrop of mountains, is an ideal site for the school of formation for all who are called to follow Jesus. The program of formation which Jesus outlines is clearly set forth in the Sermon on the Mount. Jesus touched upon many aspects of Christian living, and in listening and striving to live his way of life we discover that these tenets are not isolated directives. They form a well integrated program of formation for the dedicated disciple.

The central theme of all Jesus' teaching is love. It is the heart of his whole formation program. The conversion and conditioning necessary for commitment to Jesus must be initiated and implemented by love.

Jesus said briefly, but unequivocally: "Love your neighbor as yourself" (Mt 22:39). He pointed to the example of the Good Samaritan, who reached out in love to the man left half-dead on the road from Jerusalem to Jericho (Lk 10:25–37).

He went on to set a higher standard of love when he insisted that we love others as we love him. "I assure you, as often as you did it for one of my least brothers, you did it for me" (Mt 25:31–40).

Next Jesus asked for a love requiring a still greater commitment. In his way of life he made it a commandment: "I give you a new commandment: Love one another. Such as my love has been for you, so must your love be for one another." (Jn 13:34)

This kind of love is also the badge of discipleship. "This is how all will know you for my disciples: your love for one another" (Jn 13:35).

In this school of formation Jesus tells what is expected of those who choose to follow him and become his disciples. It is not enough merely to love family and friends, but we must also love our enemies.

> My command to you is: love your enemies, pray for your persecutors. This will prove that you are sons of your heavenly Father, for his sun rises on the bad and the good, he rains on the just and the unjust. If you love those who love you, what merit is there in that? Do not tax collectors do as much? And if you greet your brothers only, what is so praiseworthy about that? Do not pagans do as much? In a word, you must be made perfect as your heavenly Father is perfect. (Mt 5:44–48)

It is not easy to love all our neighbors and even more difficult to reach out in love to enemies. Says G.K. Chesterton: "Of course, that is because they are the same people." Jesus not only required this kind of love, he also demonstrated it for us. Throughout his life he was gentle and patient with his enemies. He could have devastated them, but instead he loved them. His love for his enemies climaxed on the cross when he prayed: "Father, forgive them; they do not know what they are doing" (Lk 23:34).

Before we can love our enemies we must be reconciled, and the basis of any reconciliation is forgiveness. In his Sermon on the Mount Jesus taught us to pray: "Forgive us the wrong we have done as we forgive those who wrong us" (Mt 6:12). Immediately after teaching us this prayer, he added, "If you forgive the faults of others, your heavenly Father will forgive you yours. If you do not forgive others, neither will your Father forgive you." (Mt 6:14–15)

Jesus wants us to be genuinely formed as his disciples, but before we can give ourselves totally to God we must be reconciled with others. "If you bring your gift to the altar and there recall that your brother has anything against you, leave your gift at the altar, go first to be reconciled with your brother, and then come and offer your gift" (Mt 5:23–24).

Jesus emphatically explains that before we can be recognized as his disciples by our love for one another, we must be reconciled with others. We must strive to forgive others and ask them to forgive us. Only then will our love begin to germinate and grow into a full-blown relationship.

Source of Love

Jesus understood perfectly that because of our human frailties we would find it difficult to love all those who cross our path on our pilgrimage through life. To enable us to love, Jesus made us temples of the Holy Spirit, who is the inexhaustible fountain of love. "The love of God has been poured out in our hearts through the Holy Spirit who has been given to us" (Rom 5:5).

We are surrounded and filled with God's love as a dry sponge dropped into the ocean and saturated with sea water. Furthermore, love has this special quality: the more we give away, the more we receive in return.

The Holy Spirit enables us to love by binding us together into the family of God. Through our baptism we become members of the Body of Christ, sharing in his divine life and becoming brothers and sisters. This is the work of the Spirit dwelling within us.

All who are led by the Spirit of God are sons [and daughters] of God. . . . The Spirit himself gives witness with our spirit that we are children of God. But if we are children, we are heirs as well: heirs of God, heirs with Christ. (Rom 8:14)

While his "new commandment" may seem difficult, Jesus has given us every means possible to support us in fulfilling it. He invites us to become channels through which he can reach out in love to others. As we permit his love to flow through us, we can more readily let our love accompany his love in touching others.

Our Father

In his Sermon on the Mount, Jesus teaches us to call the transcendent God of heaven and earth, the almighty, powerful Creator of the whole universe, Father—our Father, my Father. In Jesus' time, such a title and claiming such a relationship was the height of blasphemy. No one would dare even insinuate such a personal bond between creature and Creator.

Jesus wants his disciples to be aware of our loving Father in our daily living, and he gave us a very practical way of doing so. He taught us the Lord's Prayer (Mt 6:9-13), which expresses our relationship with our Father and our dependence on him. It reminds us that we are his children, and he is our loving Father.

After calling God our Father, we plead, "Hallowed be your name," asking that God be honored, worshipped, and respected as the transcendent God of heaven and earth; even more, that we recognize and love him as our gracious, loving Father. We pray that in our own lives we may praise and glorify his name. We also pray that through our lifestyle many persons may come to give him the worship, glory, and praise which we all owe him.

"Your kingdom come" is a fervent prayer that we and all creation may be open and receptive to the divine life with which he wishes to fill us. This kingdom is his indwelling in us, with his divine life and love, which can be effected only partially in this life, but more fully in the life to come. This is what heaven is all about—a total union of love with our Father.

The petition "your will be done on earth as it is in heaven" reminds us of Jesus, who was solely concerned with doing the will of the Father at all times and in all circumstances. How plainly he said, "I am not seeking my own will but the will of him who sent me" (Jn 5:30). The will of the Father, precisely fulfilled, totally preoccupied him, it was his whole motivation: "Doing the will of him who sent me and bringing his work to completion is my food" (Jn 4:34). This determination climaxed in the Garden of Gethsemane: "Father, if it is your will, take this cup from me; yet not my will but yours be done" (Lk 22:42).

In the second portion of the Lord's Prayer, Jesus assures us that his Father is a provident Father who loves us and cares for us at every moment of the day, providing all our spiritual and temporal needs. To remind us of our Father's care, and our dependence on it, Jesus taught us to pray: "Give us today our daily bread."

This petition is addressed to the Father as our provider. It is a prayer for the present — "this day." We might even abbreviate it to "Give us this day."

Jesus taught about the providential love of the Father in some detail and drew a convincing illustration: If a human father wants to give only good things to his children, "how much more will your heavenly Father give good things to anyone who asks him!" (Mt 7:11). We must implicitly trust him, for Jesus assures us: "Your heavenly Father knows all that you need" (Mt 6:32).

The second petition which follows it is addressed to God as our Savior and Redeemer: "Forgive us the wrong we have done as we forgive those who wrong us." This petition is directed toward our past, far removed or immediate. Jesus came to be our Redeemer and our Healer. It is true that we say he is off in his glory; but what is his glory? His glory is continuing his redemptive work in us.

We may be concerned about the extent of our own forgiveness toward others. The words "as we forgive those who wrong us" may disturb us. We know from personal experience that we have often tried to forgive and forget, but find it very difficult.

Again the compassionate understanding of God assures us that if we *want* to forgive, he accepts it as forgiveness. We cannot accomplish anything without his gift. If we could forgive completely, without reservation, it would be his gift. Paul assures us: "It is God who, in his good will toward you, begets in you any measure of desire or achievement" (Phil 2:13).

Next we pray: "Subject us not to the trial, but deliver us from the evil one."

When Jesus died on the cross he handed over the work of sanctification to the Holy Spirit. As the source of divine love living within us, he is encouraging us, strengthening us, guiding us with his gifts of wisdom, knowledge, understanding, and discernment. These gifts of the Spirit help us to recognize the wiles of the evil one. They enable us to keep our focus on the Lord and strengthen us in maintaining our fundamental decision to serve the Lord and him alone.

The Lord's Prayer is not merely a private prayer. The very words are communal. "Our Father...give us...our daily bread... forgive us...subject us not to the trial." We pray in the plural. We pray with our Christian brothers and sisters as the People of God.

Jesus calls us to the Mount of Beatitudes not primarily to teach us a communal prayer to memorize. Rather, each phrase calls us to conversion and commitment. This is a prayer we must live. Our brief respite on the Mount begins the formation which will enable us to live in the spirit of the Lord's Prayer.

In this aspect of our spiritual formation, as well as in all other aspects, Jesus is our model, our exemplar. He lived his commitment to the Father's salvific plan. Furthermore, he takes us by the hand and bids us follow him: "I am the way, and the truth, and the life; no one comes to the Father but through me" (Jn 14:6).

The Golden Rule

Perhaps the most famous teaching of Jesus in the Sermon on the Mount is, "Treat others the way you would have them treat you: this sums up the law and the prophets" (Mt 7:12).

With this commandment, which has been called the capstone of the whole discourse, the Sermon reaches its climax. We can find many parallels of it in literature before and during Jesus' time. However, Jesus gave it a different direction. All previous sayings were in the negative. For example, "What is hateful to yourself, do to no others" (Shammai Rabbi). Epictetus put it this way: "What you avoid suffering yourself, seek not to inflict upon others." Even Psalm 15 states this Golden Rule in the negative. The negative form of the rule involves nothing more than not doing certain things which might be harmful to others. By stating the Golden Rule in the positive, Jesus called us to go out of our way to help other people and be kind to them, as we would wish them to help us and be kind to us. Only love can compel us to do this.

"I must do no harm to others" is quite different from "I must do my best to help others."

Commitment

Jesus calls us to the Mount of Beatitudes. He invites us to follow him. He calls us into discipleship. He urges us to "come and see" what his way is all about. Only then does he ask for our commitment.

Jesus explains how tragic it would be for us to come and listen to his words, but fail to put them into practice. We may be like the man in the Gospel. Jesus advised this man, who wanted to follow him, to "go and sell what you have and give to the poor; you will then have treasure in heaven. After that, come and follow me." And the evangelist concludes: "He went away sad for he had many possessions" (Mk 10:21).

Jesus makes an apt comparison. He says:

Anyone who hears my words but does not put them into practice is like the foolish man who built his house on sandy ground. The rains fell, the torrents came, the winds blew and lashed against his house. It collapsed under all this and was completely ruined. (Mt 7:26–27)

Jesus describes the ministry of a devoted disciple who has sat at his feet and allowed his words to transform him.

Anyone who hears my words and puts them into practice is like the wise man who built his house on rock. When the rainy season set in, the torrents came and the winds blew and buffeted his house. It did not collapse; it had been solidly built on rock. (Mt 7:24–25)

All of us, I am sure, would love to stay here on the Mount of Beatitudes, to listen to the birds singing, to hang on every word which Jesus proclaims. However, Jesus must be on his way and so must we.

When Jesus called us into discipleship he told us, "You are the light of the world" (Mt 5:14). We must be about our mission in life and let our light shine before men.

> In the same way, your light must shine before men so that they may see goodness in your acts and give praise to your heavenly Father. (Mt 5:16)

We climbed the Mount of Beatitudes with expectant hearts. Now nourished with Jesus' gentle instruction and formation, we descend joyous and light-footed to proclaim the Good News by our words and our lives.

SIX

Mount of Surrender and Splendor

This is my Son, my Chosen One. Listen to him.

(Lk 9:35)

THE NEXT STEP in the process of spiritual growth and maturation requires another mountain-climbing expedition. There is an important dimension in our spiritual development, difficult to understand and even more difficult to accept unless we walk in step with Jesus. Jesus invites us to climb Mount Tabor with him.

A gorgeous place it is. Mount Tabor is a sugar loaf mountain in the plain of Esdraelon. Its summit is 1,500 feet above the valley floor—a perfect altar, canopied by the vault of heaven, in this sanctuary of the Holy Land. This is one of the most picturesque places in all of Israel, with a stunning view of the fertile valley below, and of Mount Hermon to the north and Mount Gerizim to the south.

A hairpinned narrow road leads to the summit of Mount Tabor. We pause to survey the exquisite beauty laid out before us. We may pause not only to rest momentarily in our ascent, but also to reflect on the surge of events in Jesus' life.

Jesus realized that his teaching mission was drawing to a close. Soon he must enter into his mission of suffering, terminating in his death. He tried to prepare himself and his disciples for this paradoxical mission of his glorious victory through dreadful defeat.

The first stage of this preparation took place at Caesarea Philippi. Jesus went with his disciples to this remote area of Palestine to be alone, away from the demanding crowds. In the solitude and quiet of this region, Jesus asked his disciples some pointed questions. He wanted them to verbalize their faith in him. They had to hear themselves expressing their own faith in him and his mission, especially his mission of suffering and death.

At Caesarea Philippi Jesus' question to his disciples was direct: "Who do you say that I am?" How pleased he was with their profession, spoken by Peter: "You are the Messiah, . . . the Son of the living God" (Mt 16:15–16).

Then Jesus began to prepare them for what awaited him as the Messiah.

> From then on Jesus, the Messiah, started to indicate to his disciples that he must go to Jerusalem and suffer greatly there at the hands of the elders, the chief priests, and the scribes, and to be put to death, and raised up on the third day. (Mt 16:21)

As was to be expected, the disciples did not understand. This was not their idea of a Messiah. They expected a great political and military leader who would free them from Roman occupation and establish them once again as a free people. With this concept uppermost in their minds the response of Peter was not surprising.

> At this, Peter took him aside and began to remonstrate with him. "May you be spared, Master! God forbid that any such thing ever happen to you!" Jesus turned on Peter and said, "Get out of my sight, you satan! You are trying to make me trip and fall. You are not judging by God's standards, but by man's."
> (Mt 16:22–23)

No doubt we would have reacted like Peter. Have we not wondered why the Lord permitted a particular pain, hardship, or misfortune in our lives? Do we not often wonder why, if God is such a good, kind, and gracious God, he allows so much suffering, violence, and injustice? Like Peter's, perhaps our idea of a Messiah does not always conform to God's idea. The Lord prepared us for this when he said, "My thoughts are not your thoughts, nor are your ways my ways" (Is 55:8).

Soon after this first prediction of his passion, Jesus reminded his disciples of the fate of the Messiah.

When they met again in Galilee, Jesus said to them, "The Son of Man is going to be delivered into the hands of men who will put him to death, and he will be raised up on the third day." At these words they were overwhelmed with grief. (Mt 17:22–23)

The disciples simply could not comprehend the idea that Jesus would ever go down in defeat. They were convinced that his Father would never permit him to suffer and die. So often he had walked untouched through the midst of his enemies (Lk 4:28–30; Jn 7:45–46).

A third time:

As Jesus was starting to go up to Jerusalem, he took the Twelve aside on the road and said to them: "We are going up to Jerusalem now. There the Son of Man will be handed over to the chief priests and scribes, who will condemn him to death. They will turn him over to the Gentiles, to be made sport of and flogged and crucified. But on the third day he will be raised up." (Mt 29:17–19)

Jesus confronted the reality of his death looming up before him. The apostles, too, would have to realize that his passion and death were permitted by the Father for the world's redemption.

There was an even greater reason for going up the mountain. Jesus never ventured on any phase of his ministry without the approval of his Father. Jesus came to Mount Tabor to seek and receive the Father's approval and strength.

The great moment of Caesarea Philippi was followed by the great hour on the Mount of Transfiguration. There Jesus went up with his three favorite apostles, Peter, James, and John. He invites us to go with him.

Why did Jesus go there? Why did he make this expedition to this lonely mountain? St. Luke writes: "He [Jesus] took Peter, John and James, and went onto a mountain to pray" (Lk 9:28).

Let us be with Jesus. He is on the way to the cross. Of this he is quite certain.

At Caesarea Philippi Jesus was dealing with a big question. He asked it in order to discover whether or not anyone had recognized him for who he really was. We heard Peter's messianic answer. But there was yet another question which Jesus had to solve before he set out on this last journey. He had to make certain, beyond any shadow of a doubt, that he was doing what his Father wished him to do. He had to make certain that it was his Father's will that he go to the cross.

Jesus always asked, "Is this your will for me, Father?" In the loneliness of that mountaintop Jesus was asking that same question of the Father: "What is it you want me to do now?"

How differently Jesus approached his mission than we do. Most of the time we ask, "What do I want to do?" or at best, "Father, come help me do what I have decided to do."

Jesus always freely chose the will of his Father. Their wills were always in accord. One of the ways we express our love is to do what we know will please our beloved. Everything Jesus did was a love-offering to the Father.

We take our place with Jesus and his three chosen apostles on the top of that gorgeous mountain. In prayer let us ask Jesus to give us, as he did his apostles, deeper insight into himself and his mission, especially his mission of suffering soon to begin.

Centuries before, the Israelites with trust in God ventured out of the slavery of Egypt into the uncharted wastes of the desert. Now Jesus was about to do the same. With complete trust in his Father, Jesus was about to set out on his journey to Jerusalem, a hazardous, uncharted journey which led to the cross and beyond to glory.

Before we accompany Jesus on his way, let us pause to experience the extraterrestrial phenomenon which took place on this mountaintop.

While he [Jesus] was praying, his face changed in appearance and his clothes became dazzlingly white. Suddenly two men were talking with him—Moses and Elijah. They appeared in glory and spoke of his passage, which he was about to fulfill in Jerusalem. (Lk 9:29-31)

The appearance of Moses and Elijah is significant. Moses was the great lawgiver, who had made known to the Israelites the way in which God wanted them to live. Elijah, one of the great prophets, revealed God's message with unique directness.

These two pillars of Israel's history now appear to Jesus as he was about to set out on his last and most important adventure. They recognized in him the fulfillment of God's plan of salvation, of which they had dreamed, and encouraged him to continue his exodus to Jerusalem and Calvary and on to glory.

Significant as this confirmation of Moses and Elijah was, it was almost obliterated by the bright cloud which overshadowed them. From that cloud came the voice of divine majesty setting the Father's approval on Jesus and what he was about to undertake: "This is my beloved Son on whom my favor rests. Listen to him." (Mt 17:5)

Throughout Israel's history a brilliant or luminous cloud signified the *shekinah*—the revelation of God. In the Book of Exodus we learn that "the column of a cloud" guided the people on their way (Ex 13:21-22) and also came to rest on the "meeting tent" (Ex 40:34). Moses met God in a cloud (Ex 34:5). Throughout the Old Testament the mysterious glory of God appears in a cloud.

The transfiguration was indeed a mountain-peak experience. Jesus' journey to Jerusalem and the waiting arms of the cross was confirmed not only by the greatest of lawgivers and prophets, but by the Father himself. All was in accord with his divine will.

It was this experience on Mount Tabor which enabled Jesus to walk the way of the cross.

The Apostles

In this theophany, this manifestation of God, the divinity of Jesus radiated through his humanity. The apostles saw Jesus in all his taboric splendor.

They needed this experience of his transcendence, for they were still hurting at Jesus' prediction of his impending death. It seemed to them utter defeat — the shattering of all their hopes and expectations of the Messiah. However, the whole experience on Mount Tabor was one of glory: "His face became as dazzling as the sun, his clothes as radiant as light" (Mt 17:2). As good Jews they understood the glorious *shekinah* of the cloud. From now on, the journey to Jerusalem and death, even though painful and puzzling, was framed in glory.

Witnessing the divine splendor also helped the apostles realize that God's ways were far beyond their imagination. If they could not comprehend the glory of God, how could they possibly understand his divine plan of salvation?

The Father had not only confirmed the mission of Jesus, but he urged the apostles to accept whatever was to take place. Imperatively the Father said: "Listen to him."

Speaking about this theophany, St. Leo the Great said:

> The great reason for this transfiguration was to remove the scandal of the cross from the hearts of the disciples, and to prevent the humiliation of his voluntary suffering from disturbing the faith of those who had witnessed the surpassing glory that lay concealed.
>
> With no less forethought he was also providing a firm foundation for the hope of the holy Church. The whole body of Christ was to understand the kind of transformation that it would receive as his gift. The members of the body were to look forward to a share in that glory which first blazed out in Christ as their head.

The Peter in Us

Peter was deeply moved by this celestial experience. He was no longer trying to dissuade Jesus from going up to Jerusalem. His response reveals how overwhelming was this experience for him: "Master, how good it is for us to be here" (Lk 9:33). Impulsive and a man of action, he went on: "Let us set up three booths, one for you, one for Moses, and one for Elijah. (He did not really know what he was saying.)" This was a time for quiet, for contemplation, for awe and wonder, for reverence and adoration; but Peter was eager to swing into action. He wanted to preserve this experience indefinitely.

Like Peter, we are often too busy, too preoccupied in the presence of the Lord. How well the psalmist advises us: "Be still and know that I am God" (Ps 46:11, Grail translation).

Peter wished to stay on the mountaintop and prolong this great moment. He did not want to return to the demands of life. He wanted to remain forever in this other-worldly glory.

All of us have had similar experiences. We have enjoyed moments of awareness of God's presence. We have experienced his love, peace, and serenity. The taboric experiences are always more enjoyable than the demanding duties of our daily routine or the pain of our own way of the cross. Mountaintop experiences provide strength, courage, motivation for our daily ministry, and prepare us also for the burdens which come our way. Moments of glory do not exist for their own sake, but to make the mundane more radiant than before.

Jesus needed to spend time in communion with his Father. This precious time for prayer strengthened, enlightened, and enabled him to acquiesce to the Father's plan of salvation. After his unconditional yes to the Father, his divinity burst forth in all its splendor.

We frequently need to "go up the mountain to pray." In prayer we meet Jesus in a personal manner which cannot take place in any other way. In a quiet prayer of listening we can experience the tenderness of his love which guides, protects, and provides for us at all times and under all circumstances. In prayer we are reminded of the Father's reassurance, "For I know well the plans I have in mind for you, . . . plans for your welfare, not for woe!" (Jer 29:11).

As we rest with Jesus on the mountaintop we discover that he permits the pinpricks of everyday living — the little crosses, hardships, misunderstandings, aches and pains — to purify, sanctify, and mature us. Daily dying to self enables us to say with St. Paul: "I consider the sufferings of the present to be as nothing compared with the glory to be revealed in us" (Rom 8:18).

Years later, when St. Peter realized that his own death was imminent, he urged us to adhere tenaciously to the truths he taught, and especially to look forward to the coming of the Lord to receive us into his glory.

> It was not by way of cleverly concocted myths that we taught you about the coming in power of our Lord Jesus Christ, for we were eyewitnesses of his sovereign majesty. He received glory and praise from God the Father when that unique declaration came to him out of the majestic splendor: "This is my beloved Son, on whom my favor rests." We ourselves heard this said from heaven while we were in his company on the holy mountain. Besides, we possess the prophetic message as something altogether reliable. Keep your attention closely fixed on it, as you would on a lamp shining in a dark place until the first streaks of dawn appear and the morning star rises in your hearts.
>
> (2 Pt 1:16–19)

Our own Tabor may be our aloneness with Jesus in prayer, our experience of the warmth of his love, our peace and joy. We descend from Mount Tabor with the memory of the splendor and glory of Jesus to fortify us as we continue our pilgrimage through life and on to our own Calvary.

Just as Jesus radiated the peace and joy of submitting completely to the will of the Father, we too must reflect that deep interior joy, which is the fruit of knowing that God loves us so much that no harm can come to us.

Our mission in life, like that of the three apostles, is to bring hope and encouragement, comfort and consolation to those who have not experienced the glory of Jesus.

Our mission is to let the taboric light shine through us, as St. Paul says:

> For God, who said, "Let light shine out of darkness," has shone in our hearts, that we in turn might make known the glory of God shining on the face of Christ. This treasure we possess in earthen vessels to make it clear that its surpassing power comes from God and not from us. (2 Cor 4:6)

SEVEN

Love's Mystery Unfolded

This is my body to be given for you. (Lk 22:19)

IN THE HISTORY of God's communicating with his people, mountains play a significant role. On mountaintops God seems to interact more personally, more frequently, and more intimately with his prophets, priests, and people.

No wonder the psalmist sings, "The tops of the mountains are his" (Ps 95:4). The massive elegance of the mountains, the commanding view from their heights, spontaneously draw us into a contemplative mood, inspiring awe and reverence for the Creator who fashioned these massive outbursts of beauty.

Since mountains have become synonymous and symbolic of God's trysting place with his people, we are not surprised to find the Cenacle situated on Mount Zion. Here God shares his life and love with us in an extraordinary manner. Here Jesus gave us himself in the Holy Eucharist. St. Luke relates the event in these words: "The day of Unleavened Bread arrived on which it was appointed to sacrifice the paschal lamb. Accordingly, Jesus sent Peter and John off with the instruction, 'Go and prepare our Passover supper for us.' " (Lk 22:7–8)

Not only did the Last Supper take place on Mount Zion, but the room prepared for this earthshaking event was an "upstairs room." High places certainly are featured in God's dealing with his creatures.

From this hallowed Upper Room, high on Mount Zion,

emanated all the love of a God who was so deeply in love with his people that he could not leave us orphans. In his divine wisdom he devised a unique way of remaining with us. He adapted himself to our human limitations by giving us signs and symbols of his abiding presence — bread and wine.

This was not a sudden impulse on the part of Jesus. He prepared us well for this magnanimous gift of himself in the Eucharist. Already he had proven his power over water at the wedding feast in Cana of Galilee. Here the modest water saw its God and blushed so profusely that it became a choice, sparkling wine.

Motivated by his loving concern for his people, Jesus manifested his power over bread by feeding a whole multitude with only "five barley loaves and a couple of dried fish" (Jn 6:9). This paved the way for that astounding announcement at Capernaum: "I myself am the bread of life. No one who comes to me shall ever be hungry, no one who believes in me shall ever thirst" (Jn 6:35). Jesus fulfilled this promise in the Upper Room the night before he died:

> During the meal Jesus took bread, blessed it, broke it, and gave it to his disciples. "Take this and eat it," he said, "this is my body." Then he took a cup, gave thanks, and gave it to them. "All of you must drink from it," he said, "for this is my blood, the blood of the covenant, to be poured out in behalf of many for the forgiveness of sins." (Mt 26:26–28)

Jesus looked forward to this moment when he would give us the gift of himself in the Eucharist. Note the eagerness in his words: "I have greatly desired to eat this Passover with you before I suffer" (Lk 22:15).

Why did Jesus sacramentalize his presence among us? Why did he want to remain with us under the appearance of bread and wine? Why did he institute the Eucharist as a sacrament and also as a sacrifice? In spirit we ascend Mount Zion and climb the steps leading into the Upper Room to ask Jesus why he gave us himself in the Eucharist.

Love

By abiding with us in such a concrete way, Jesus speaks to us of his infinite love. He promised: "I will not leave you orphaned; I will come back to you" (Jn 14:18).

Love longs to be close to the person loved, to share in the joys and sorrows of the beloved. If this is true of human love, which is often self-centered and imperfect, how much more so of divine love.

All that Jesus asks is that we open ourselves to his love by striving to live the lifestyle which he taught us, both by his word and by his example. We can sense his eagerness to abide with us: "Anyone who loves me will be true to my word, and my Father will love him; we will come to him and make our dwelling place with him" (Jn 14:23).

Food for the Journey

No destination is safely reached without provisions for all the needs along the way. Automobiles need to be refueled from time to time. Bodies need to be replenished with food and drink several times a day. We need sustenance on our journey heavenward. Jesus gave himself in the Eucharist to nourish us on our way back to the Father. "For my flesh is real food and my blood real drink. The man who feeds on my flesh and drinks my blood remains in me, and I in him." (Jn 6:55–56)

Jesus is the manna in our wasteland and the gushing spring of fresh water in the desert. When people asked for ordinary bread, he explained:

> You shall not be working for perishable food but for food that remains unto life eternal, food which the Son of Man will give you. . . . I myself am the bread of life. No one who comes to me shall ever be hungry, no one who believes in me shall ever thirst. (Jn 6:27, 35)

Jesus supplies us with all the spiritual mega-vitamins we need to ward off any evil threatening us. He strengthens us to pull our share of his yoke. He invigorates us to daily carry our cross.

His presence is also healing. Friends are a healing presence in time of stress or pain. Jesus dwelling with us is a healing presence in trial and temptation, in misunderstanding and misfortune.

How healing was his presence in the Cenacle when he spoke during that Last Supper:

> Do not let your hearts be troubled. Have faith in God and faith in me. In my Father's house there are many dwelling places; otherwise how could I have told you that I was going to prepare a place for you? I am indeed going to prepare a place for you, and then I shall come back to take you with me, that where I am you also may be. You know the way that leads where I go.... I will ask the Father and he will give you another Paraclete—to be with you always. (Jn 14:1–4, 16)

His prayer is consoling and comforting and always heard:

> Father, all those you gave me I would have in my company where I am. (Jn 17:24)

The healing love of Jesus radiates from his eucharistic presence, a soothing balm on our earthly sojourn. St. Thomas says:

> No other sacrament has greater healing power, through it sins are purged away, virtues are increased, and the soul is enriched with an abundance of every spiritual gift.
>
> (Feast of Corpus Christi)

Our Companion

A good companion makes a journey more pleasant and delightful. Jesus accompanied the disciples to Emmaus and gave them hope and comfort as he explained the scriptures to them. They asked each other, "Were not our hearts burning inside us as he talked to us on the road and explained the Scriptures to us?" (Lk 24:32).

On our journey through life we may be uncertain of the way. We come to many crossroads and may wonder which way to turn. We need guidance and direction. We need a companion to help us discover and discern God's will for us, especially his will of preference. We need confirmation and support on our pilgrimage back to the Father. Jesus, aware of our need, assures us in his eucharistic presence that he is always with us.

As He becomes Eucharist for us, he helps us not only to learn the will of his Father, but also strengthens and encourages us to do it. His own life is a paradigm for us to imitate. When our path seems rough and rocky, he is there, guiding our footsteps lest we stumble and fall. When the hills seem high and the valleys deep, Jesus is there to lift our spirits, to take us by the hand and support us. When the load we carry seems intolerably heavy, he relieves the burden and shows us how useless are many of the things we are trying to take with us.

Always, when we get discouraged or disheartened, when the journey seems long and tiresome, Jesus is there to fix our vision on the top of the mountain. He reminds us of the joy and peace awaiting us.

The Eucharist is a mysterious dimension of Incarnate Love, a concrete expression of the Lord's abiding, providential, enduring love enveloping us at all times. Coming to us in Holy Communion, he reminds us that he is always and everywhere our companion.

As we contemplate this mystery of Jesus' love for us, we make our own the psalmist's prayer:

> How shall I make a return to the Lord
>   for all the good he has done for me?
> The cup of salvation I will take up,
>   and I will call upon the name of the Lord. . . .
> To you will I offer sacrifice of thanksgiving,
>   and I will call upon the name of the Lord. (Ps 116:12–13, 17)

"How shall I make a return to the Lord?" Jesus answers that question. He wants us to be his "other self." Jesus becomes Eucharist for us. Now he asks us to become Eucharist to all those whose lives we touch in loving concern, for Jesus radiates through us in all our attitudes and actions.

The disciples on the road to Emmaus gave us the example. Jesus brought them hope and consolation, reassuring them he was risen and alive, as the prophets had foretold. Their mission was to spread the Good News of the Resurrection: "They got up immediately and returned to Jerusalem, where they found the Eleven and the rest of the company assembled. . . . They recounted what had happened on the road and how they had come to know him in the breaking of bread." (Lk 24:33, 35) They were transformed from disappointed, dejected disciples into emissaries of joy as they spread the Good News.

Each time we offer the Eucharist and give ourselves more generously to Jesus, his transforming love helps us to "put on that new man created in God's image" (Eph 4:24).

We gaze in awe and wonder at the mystery of his eucharistic love: "All of us, gazing on the Lord's glory with unveiled faces, are being transformed from glory to glory into his very image by the Lord who is the Spirit" (2 Cor 3:18). And as the fruits of this transformation mature in us, we bring the Good News to all we meet.

We do not come to the Eucharist alone. The eucharistic sacrifice is a corporate act of the whole Body of Christ — all our brothers and sisters united with Jesus. We bring our family and friends and those for whom we pray, and with the gift of ourselves we offer them to our loving Father through the mediation of our eternal high priest, Jesus.

As we grow and mature in God's life and love, we become his witnesses. In the Gospel Jesus called the disciples: "Come," "Come and see," and "Come, follow me." Only after they had put on his mind and heart did he commission them to "go and make disciples of all the nations" (Mt 28:19).

He invites us to be transformed by the Eucharist and to become Eucharist to others. This is the meaning of the church's bidding to us at the end of Mass: "Go in the peace of Christ" or "The Mass is ended, go in peace" or "Go in peace to love and serve the Lord." It is varied from day to day so that it doesn't become a trite expression.

On our journey to our own Emmaus, be it at home or elsewhere, we meet the weary and heavily burdened who may not know Jesus as we know him, or who do not know him at all. Jesus wants us to represent him along the way, to present him to them by living the Good News and keeping "our hearts burning inside us."

Do This As a Remembrance of Me

The greatest prayer and most sublime act of worship is the Eucharistic Celebration.

Jesus, when he gave us himself in the Eucharist, told us to pray and worship in this manner, saying "Do this as a remembrance of me" (Lk 22:19). But what does this really mean? We must not interpret this invitation of Jesus too narrowly. Jesus meant much more than the words of consecration.

Have you heard the excuse, "I don't go to Mass any more because I don't get anything out of it"? We do not offer the Eucharist to "get something out of it." Jesus did not *get* very much when he struggled on to Calvary, but he *gave* an awful lot! In fact, he gave everything.

The Mass is an oblation, a privileged opportunity to give ourselves and all that we do and are to our Father in heaven. It is our unique prerogative to be in direct communication with the transcendent God of heaven and earth.

In this celebration Jesus invites us to bring the gift of ourselves, effectively represented by the bread and wine. He unites our gift with the gift of himself to the Father, making our gift, even though it may be self-centered, half-hearted at times, take on a new and infinite dimension.

The Father graciously accepts our gift with the oblation of Jesus himself. When Jesus directs us to "do this as a remembrance of me," he is inviting us to put on his mind, his heart, his attitudes, so that our lives conform to his. Then our gift is pleasing to the Father.

Our interior dispositions are all-important. "Yet an hour is coming, and is already here, when authentic worshippers will worship the Father in Spirit and truth" (Jn 4:23).

Jesus linked the Old Testament idea of worshipping God with all one's heart, mind, and soul to the love of neighbor, and included the love of neighbor in making our oblation: "If you bring your gift to the altar and there recall that your brother has anything against you, leave your gift at the altar, go first to be reconciled with your brother, and then come and offer your gift" (Mt 5:23–24).

He also asks us to offer ourselves and all our personal relationships to the Father in the Eucharist, where they will be healed and the bonds perfected by the outpouring of his love upon us.

Jesus, our model, our exemplar, shows us the way. From the first moment of his birth in Bethlehem up to his last gasp on the cross, Jesus gave himself to his Father. Unless we unite our own self-giving with the self-giving of Jesus, the Mass and its words remain empty, devoid of any meaning or fruit.

Many people think of the words of consecration as the precise moment when Jesus begins to be eucharistically present in our midst. Yet there is a long-standing agreement among theologians and liturgists that the whole eucharistic prayer is consecratory.

St. John spent one-fourth of his Gospel on the last discourse of Jesus and never even describes the supper itself. Though John may not have mentioned the words of consecration, he does stress the dispositions which are necessary. He begins his account with Jesus washing the feet of the apostles, to welcome them, to cleanse them, to prepare them for the spiritual food which he was about to give them. Jesus gave. He was in their midst as one who serves.

We miss the whole point of the eucharistic sacrifice if we miss the example and words of Jesus: "I give you a new commandment: love one another." And to what extent? "Such as my love has been for you, so must your love be for each other" (Jn 13:34).

A practical, operative love, then, is the essence of the Eucharist. "Do this as a remembrance of me" are not mere words, nor a call to a formal ritual ceremony only, but a call to give as Jesus gave. It means giving ourselves totally and entirely as Jesus gave himself.

This kind of loving service is brought to the altar with the gift which Jesus is making of himself on our behalf. We worship "in Spirit and truth" when the eucharistic ritual conforms and expresses a life lived for others. To expect otherwise is to attach magical powers of transformation to our participation in the Eucharist.

Ultimately, worship is not something we do and then offer to God; but rather it is something we are—the image of Jesus which has been formed in us. In each Eucharistic Celebration the transcendent God becomes more immanent, transforming our humanness into his divine image. His coming expands our capacity to receive a more abundant influx of his divine life. Then we can become eucharist to others, radiating his divine life and love.

Surely we are chosen souls: "It was not you who chose me, it was I who chose you to go forth and bear fruit" (Jn 15:16). And what joy in the fulfillment of the prophecy of Malachi: "From the rising of the sun, even to its setting, my name is great among the nations; and everywhere they bring sacrifice to my name, and a pure offering" (Mal 1:11).

Healing

We ascend Mount Zion and climb the stairs into the Upper Room to offer the Eucharist with Jesus, and we experience it as a sacrament of healing. Jesus came to be our healer. He healed not so much to prove his divine power but to manifest his great love for us. He healed because he loved.

Jesus left us a legacy of healing in his Word. The Gospels are replete with accounts of his healing love: "The blind recover their sight, cripples walk, lepers are cured, the deaf hear, dead men are raised to life, and the poor have the good news preached to them" (Mt 11:5).

Jesus came as our Savior and Healer. Now, in his glory at the right hand of the Father, he continues his redemptive, healing mission among us.

Furthermore, he is happy we ask his healing power, because we are permitting him to be what he wants to be most—Savior and Redeemer. Our coming to him means we are receptive to the transformation he wants to effect within us.

Jesus promised: "Know that I am with you always, until the end of the world" (Mt 28:20). He is dynamically present within us as we encounter him in his sacraments, the channels of his healing love operative within us. Special channels of healing are the

Eucharist, baptism, reconciliation, and the anointing of the sick. The Mass as a whole is not only a prayer of healing, but the very source of the healing power and love of Jesus for us.

Prayer for Healing and Forgiveness

In the penitential rite of the Mass we beg God's forgiveness and healing. In the sunshine of his presence, we can see ourselves more clearly. Our human weaknesses, our pride, our self-centeredness, our unwillingness to reach out in love, our lack of joyous submission to his will, all loom up before us as we come before the Lord. In humility and sorrow we turn to him: "Lord have mercy, Christ have mercy, Lord have mercy."

Next we pray: "May Almighty God have mercy on us, forgive us our sins and lead us to life everlasting."

Later on in the Mass we pray in the Lord's Prayer: "Forgive us our trespasses. . . . lead us not into temptation. . . ."

The prayer which follows the Our Father is also a beautiful prayer for healing: "Deliver us, Lord, from every evil and grant us peace in our day. In your mercy keep us from sin and protect us from all anxiety as we wait in joyful hope for the coming of our Savior, Jesus Christ."

Likewise the two preparatory prayers for Holy Communion are fervent prayers for healing: "Lamb of God, you take away the sins of the world, have mercy on us" and "Lord, I am not worthy to receive you, but only say the word, and I shall be healed."

Liturgy of the Word

The Liturgy of the Word is a powerful prayer for healing. Paul sums it up in these few words: "All Scripture is inspired of God and is useful for teaching—for reproof, correction, and training in holiness so that the man of God may be fully competent and equipped for every good work" (2 Tm 3:16).

As we listen to the Word of God many things happen to us. God's Word brings us confidence and trust. It keeps us aware of his abiding love.

Our Lord himself tells us how powerful his Word can be in our lives:

> For just as from the heavens
> the rain and snow come down
> And do not return there
> till they have watered the earth
> making it fertile and fruitful....
> So shall my word be
> that goes forth from my mouth;
> It shall not return to me void,
> but shall do my will,
> achieving the end for which I sent it. (Is 55:10–11)

Sacred Scripture also has the power to heal. It can effect a conversion within us. It has the power to cleanse and change us.

> Indeed, God's word is living and effective, sharper than any two-edged sword. It penetrates and divides soul and spirit, joints and marrow; it judges the reflections and thoughts of the heart. Nothing is concealed from him; all lies bare and exposed to the eyes of him to whom we must render an account.
>
> (Heb 4:12–13)

Sometimes this conversion is painless, since God's Word transforms our heart without our even being aware of it. We may become more lovingly concerned about others, or more patient, or more joyous, without our even being conscious of it.

Our purpose in life is to put on the image of Jesus, to "acquire a fresh, spiritual way of thinking. You must put on that new man created in God's image." (Eph 4:23–24)

Since the scriptures reveal the personality of Jesus, a transformation takes place within all who listen to them in faith — a putting on the "new man," which is Jesus.

As we observe the loving concern of Jesus for the poor and helpless, we become more empathetic. As we reflect on his patience in dealing with his hearers, with his enemies who were trying to ensnare him, we, too, become more tolerant and patient.

This is the dynamism and power of his Word.

Liturgy of the Eucharist

Like the Liturgy of the Word, the Eucharistic Liturgy also heals. There is a healing balm in a loving personal presence. We experience this when a friend or loved one comes to visit with us, especially when we are lonely or discouraged. How much truer is it of Jesus' presence.

In the Eucharist Jesus confirms his overwhelming love for us. He could not leave us; therefore, he was eager and anxious to give himself to us in this tangible manner: "I have greatly desired to eat this Passover with you before I suffer" (Lk 22:15).

As we prepare to celebrate the Eucharist, he repeats those same words. His desire to be with us reminds us that we are loved and lovable. How often we need to hear that!

Jesus further instructed us: "Do this in remembrance of me" (Lk 22:19). He wants us to offer the Eucharist so that he can nourish us and strengthen us to ward off the subtle onslaughts of the evil one. Nurtured by his divine life we will not be hurt or wounded by insults, misunderstandings, and criticism.

Jesus knew that we would need courage, inspiration, and perseverance to fulfill the duties of each day. He assures us that we are not working alone, that he is living within us at every moment of the day.

Our goal in life is to die to self and surrender in love to God, totally giving ourselves to him. Jesus knew that this would be difficult for us; but offers us his life as an example. Jesus gave his whole life to the Father, and it culminated in this sacrificial gift of himself in the Eucharist. He is asking us to do the same.

His real presence in the Eucharist is the spiritual food we need to revitalize us. It gives us the strength and stamina to continue our pilgrimage up every mountain. Our daily spiritual ascent to the Cenacle atop of Mount Zion makes all other mountain climbing easier, even a joy.

How shall I make a return to the Lord
  for all the good he has done for me?
The cup of salvation I will take up,
  and I will call upon the name of the Lord. (Ps 116:12-13)

EIGHT

To Calvary and Glory

He shall be raised high and greatly exalted. (Is 52:13)

JESUS FIRST INVITES US to "come and see." Only after we have discovered who he is, what he teaches, and what he asks of us does he call us to "come, follow me."

Jesus did not promise that our journey through life would be a smooth superhighway with every convenience at our command. On the contrary, he prepared us for the folly of the cross:

> The message of the cross is complete absurdity to those who are headed for ruin, but to us who are experiencing salvation it is the power of God.... For God's folly is wiser than men, and his weakness more powerful than men. (1 Cor 1:18, 25)

Frequently, Jesus tried to prepare us for the price of discipleship.

> Whoever wishes to be my follower must deny his very self, take up his cross each day, and follow in my steps. Whoever would save his life will lose it, and whoever loses his life for my sake will save it. What profit does he show who gains the whole world and destroys himself in the process? (Lk 9:23–25)

Each day the Lord asks us to die to self. This process fashions the cross we are to bear throughout our earthly sojourn. Jesus set a pattern for us by continuously dying to self throughout his life on earth.

Then came the crucial test when Jesus had to live out this determination in fulfilling the Father's will. The Gospels reveal the terrible suffering he had to endure in being falsely accused, unjustly judged, totally rejected. The pain was beyond physical endurance, yet love compelled him to go on.

The merciful love of Jesus compelled him to take up his cross and trudge his painful way to Calvary. As we journey with Jesus along the Via Dolorosa, he assures us that he wanted to give himself completely for our redemption, because his love could not be satisfied with anything less.

> The Father loves me for this: that I lay down my life to take it up again. No one takes it from me; I lay it down freely. I have power to lay it down, and I have power to take it up again.
>
> (Jn 10:17–18)

Contemplating God's compassionate love for us, St. Catherine of Siena addressed the Father:

> Moved by love and wishing to reconcile the human race to yourself, you gave us your only-begotten Son. He became our mediator and our justice by taking on all our injustice and sin out of obedience to your will, eternal Father, just as you willed that he take our human nature. What an immeasurably profound love! Your Son went down from the heights of his divinity to the depths of our humanity. Can anyone's heart remain closed and hardened after this?

Jesus assures us that, given the fortunes of life, our journey in this land of exile will lead us also up a thorny path to our own Calvary, and that because of his death and resurrection, we will not be trudging our way of the cross alone. He will be there to comfort and support us every step of the way.

By his own example Jesus showed us how we are to follow him. Yet his way of the cross is not only our roadmap, but also the means by which he gives us his loving support and strength. Jesus, by his rising from the dead, is able to live with us and within us here and now. He invites us to begin anew our faltering and feeble steps toward the Calvary of our lives. He recalls for us all the humiliations, the sufferings he was willing to endure so that he could redeem our fallen human nature. Let us climb Mount Calvary with the risen Jesus.

First Station

With the risen Jesus let us relive that first stage of his torturous climb to Calvary. After the ludicrous and false accusations, "Pilate handed Jesus over to be crucified" (Jn 19:16).

As we linger with the Lord we see that living according to his way invites hostility from others. Jesus, after a lifetime of reaching out in love to every person he met, heard Caiaphas, the highpriest, ask, " 'What is your verdict?' They answered, 'He deserves death!' " (Mt 26:66) We can be certain that our secularistic society will react with hostility toward us in the same way. We may not hear anyone shriek, "Crucify him! Crucify him!" but we will be aware of undertones of criticism, ridicule, misunderstanding, and even hostility and persecution. This is to be expected, for Jesus warned us: "They will harry you as they harried me" (Jn 15:20). He also said this harassment, when it comes our way, will be to our advantage. "Blest are you when they insult you and persecute you and utter every kind of slander against you because of me. Be glad and rejoice, for your reward is great in heaven." (Mt 5:11)

Second Station

Jesus insisted that if we are going to be his followers we have to take up our cross each day and follow in his steps. He made the cross the condition of discipleship. But he showed us the way. "In the end, Pilate handed Jesus over to be crucified. Jesus was led away, and carrying the cross by himself, went out to what is called the Place of the Skull." (Jn 19:16–17)

Our cross may not be a rough, cumbersome, splintery beam. It will probably be those daily duties which can seem monotonous and unappreciated. Our dying to self may also be accepting others and being available to them when they need us. Daily dying to self in myriad different ways forms the cross we are to carry.

As we face our daily cross, Jesus reassures our hearts: "Come to me, all you who are weary and find life burdensome, and I will refresh you....for my yoke is easy and my burden light." (Mt 11:28, 30)

As we accept our cross we can be certain that Jesus smiles his approval, as he himself shoulders most of the weight of it.

Third Station

Trudging our weary way Calvary-ward, our weakened human nature may rebel. Fatigue engenders discouragement. Exhaustion seeks recompense. Self-pity soon overcomes us. These are moments of likely failure, of momentarily departing from our fundamental decision to faithfully follow in his footsteps. We may take off on a tangent to the right or to the left.

When we rationalize and excuse ourselves our fall is imminent, and after a fall our wounded pride often projects guilt onto someone or something else.

Jesus, weakened and exhausted, fell on that bloodstained trek to Golgotha, but his determination to do the Father's will enabled him to rise and continue stumbling his painful way to the place of execution.

When we sin and say no to his love, Jesus encourages us by his example to recognize our own poverty, to admit our human weakness, and to ask for his forgiveness. When we make the slightest attempt to rise from our fall, he is there to lift the yoke of our humanness by his merciful, compassionate, forgiving love. He assumes the major portion.

Our falls and our risings help us to recognize our weakness, to grow in humility, to mature spiritually, and to deepen our personal relationship with our loving Lord.

Fourth Station

From childhood days we know the healing power of a mother's love. How we would run to our mother, tears streaming down our face, when we were hurt! How healing was her tender embrace! How soothing was her kiss on the wounded area.

Mary is our spiritual Mother. She knows the pain of constantly dying to self and surrendering in love to God. She understands our struggle in acquiescing to the Father's will.

Mary had already experienced the sword of Simeon's prophecy. Now the sword of sorrow was to pierce her heart once again. As she met Jesus along his climb to Calvary, all she could do was to look at her Son. How eloquent was that look! Mary's wordless message conveyed to Jesus her willingness to make the complete oblation of herself to the Father along with him. Jesus' gaze at his Mother communicated how grateful he was to find her there.

Mary is our sorrowful Mother. She is also a healer. She accompanies us as daily we trudge our weary way of the cross. She is eager and anxious to offer us a Mother's tender assistance.

Fifth Station

We are an interdependent community-people. We are encouraged when someone reaches out to us with loving concern.

Simon the Cyrenean was unwillingly drafted into helping Jesus carry his cross. When a Roman soldier laid the blunt side of his spear on anyone's shoulder it meant that this person was being drafted into the service of the Roman government.

If possible, Simon would have avoided this humiliating commission. However, even though he shouldered the weight of the cross reluctantly, grace so touched him that it soon became more and more a labor of love.

How grateful Jesus must have been for Simon's assistance! Jesus also wanted to show us how much we need others if we are going to carry our cross successfully. Our loving Father is "the God of all consolation! He comforts us in our afflictions and thus enables us to comfort those who are in trouble, with the same consolation we have received from him." (2 Cor 1:3-4)

Even though we encounter many hills and valleys on our journey through life, we can be certain that our provident Father will have a Simon standing by to help us bear our burden.

Sixth Station

Good women are compassionate, empathetic, and sensitive. They respond generously and with loving concern. In times of need they are courageous, risking danger and hostility, even braving open opposition to be of service.

Veronica risked harm to herself to bring temporary relief to Jesus by presenting him with a cloth to wipe the blood, dirt, and spittle from his sacred face.

On our laborious journey we often need the tender, loving concern of others to assuage our pain, to encourage us when the journey seems arduous and endless, to motivate us to persevere regardless of the odds.

Jesus promised: "Know that I am with you always, until the end of the world!" (Mt 28:20). He comes to us through others. Family and friends can sooth our suffering by their loving concern. Jesus channels his love to us through our loved ones and through those in health care professions.

Yes, Jesus is walking with us at every step of the way.

Seventh Station

Beware of discouragement! The evil one uses this vulnerability as his trump card. When discouraged we give up and refuse to even try.

The clamoring of the unsympathetic crowd crescendoed when, in utter exhaustion, Jesus crumpled to the ground and lay helpless in the dirt and filth of the street. He must have been tempted to give up. But he went on. Jesus was determined to complete the total outpouring of himself that he had set out to do. We can imagine him rising himself to his elbow and pushing himself up on his knees, the executioners jerking him to his feet and driving him on.

Jesus knew how much his rising after his second fall would encourage us, especially at times when our best efforts seem futile, our intentions misunderstood, our undertakings a total failure.

Jesus motivates us by his example and by his risen presence; he picks us up, buoys up our spirits, gives us new vision, shoulders most of the burden of our cross. "Come to me, all you who are weary and find life burdensome, and I will refresh you" (Mt 11:28).

Eighth Station

"A great crowd of people followed him, including women who beat their breasts and lamented over him" (Lk 23:27). Jesus was pleased to meet the women along the way of the cross. He appreciated their loving concern.

These women could not restrain their sympathetic tears, which must have consoled Jesus in the midst of this otherwise hostile mob.

Jesus was not concerned about himself. He did not complain about the injustice, the humiliation, or the cruel inhuman treatment. As always, his concern was for others. He tried to prepare these women for what was to come because of the rejection he had received. "Daughters of Jerusalem, do not weep for me. Weep for yourselves and for your children. . . . If they do these things in the green wood, what will happen in the dry?" (Lk 23:28, 31)

Jesus accompanies us every step of the way of our pilgrimage to our Father. He anticipates our needs. He is the source of our comfort and consolation in different times.

The loving concern of our brothers and sisters in the Body of Christ is another channel through which Jesus pours out his love upon us.

Ninth Station

Painfully crushing was the third fall of Jesus under his cross. His stamina depleted, he could now see the place of execution. As he collapsed, the dirt of the street ground into his open wounds.

Suffering is a mystery in life which will forever keep its own secret. We can quite objectively speculate on the reason for suffering and pain, sickness and death and not be very disturbed. However, when severe pain wracks our own body, when infirmities restrict or hamper completely our movements, when the sword of sorrow rends our hearts, then in anguish we cry out: "Why? Why me?"

A brief visit with Jesus at this ninth station takes the focus off ourselves and enables us to unite our suffering with his mysterious passion. In our prayer Jesus' hand soothes our feverish brow. His gentle touch raises us up. The tenderness in his eyes reassures us that it is not in vain.

Listen again as he says: "And know that I am with you always, until the end of the world" (Mt 28:20). Pray that St. Paul's insight may become ours: "I consider the sufferings of the present to be as nothing compared with the glory to be revealed in us" (Rom 8:18).

Tenth Station

Our culture is a grasping one. Advertising tries to convince us of many wants—real or imagined. The world's standard of success is measured by the amount of material possessions we have or can control.

Added to this cultural influence is our own selfish human nature with all its desires. We are never satisfied. As soon as one desire is fulfilled, another one clamors for satisfaction.

With the risen Jesus at our side, we rest at the tenth station to behold Jesus being stripped of everything, even his tunic woven in one piece from top to bottom without seam (Jn 19:23). Earlier Jesus said: "The foxes have lairs, the birds of the sky have nests, but the Son of Man has nowhere to lay his head" (Lk 9:58).

Detachment frees us from worries, anxieties, and concerns which would otherwise preoccupy our time, attention, and energy. "Go and sell what you have and give to the poor; you will then have treasure in heaven. After that, come and follow me" (Mk 10:21).

Eleventh Station

Detachment culminates in total submission to God's will, regardless of what he may ask. Giving up our own will to yield graciously and generously to whatever God wants at times requires heroic efforts.

This submission is based on genuine humility. It does not create a martyr-complex, nor does it admit self-pity. It honestly says, "Your will be done."

In the eleventh station, when Jesus was nailed to the cross, he not only submitted to the will of the Father, but to the sadistic whims of his creatures. He could have devastated them, but instead "like a lamb led to the slaughter or a sheep before the shearers, he was silent and opened not his mouth" (Is 53:7).

We feel threatened if someone questions our motives or challenges our opinions. We insist that our method of doing something is the best. In prayer we try to bend God's will to coincide with our own. How earnestly we need to pray: "Your will be done."

Twelfth Station

We look at a crucifix and hear Jesus say, "There is no greater love than this: to lay down one's life for one's friends" (Jn 15:13).

Love by its very nature must be translated into action. Love gives in proportion of its depth and maturity. The divine love which overflowed the heart of Jesus could not be satisfied until it had given everything, down to the very last drop of his precious blood.

The cross is a sign of suffering and death. It is also the greatest expression of love we can imagine.

God reminded us through Hosea: "I drew them with human cords, with bands of love; I fostered them like one who raises an infant to his cheeks" (Hos 11:4).

Jesus himself foretold: "And I — once I am lifted up from earth — will draw all men to myself" (Jn 12:32).

And from the throne of his cross: "Father, forgive them; they do not know what they are doing" (Lk 23:34); "There is your mother" (Jn 19:27); "This day you will be with me in paradise" (Lk 23:43); "Father, into your hands I commend my spirit" (Lk 23:46).

In the Shadow of the Cross

The cross of Jesus is eternal. Already in the Garden of Eden our compassionate Father promised redemption to our first parents after they had sinned. He assured them that the power of the evil one would be destroyed. Eden is a tragic story with a happy ending.

The prophets kept alive the hope and expectation which eventually led to the cross. In the last of the four Servant-of-the-Lord oracles, Isaiah foreshadowed the cross: "See, my servant shall prosper, he shall be raised high and greatly exalted.... And he shall take away the sins of many, and win pardon for their offenses." (Is 52:13; 53:12)

All that had gone on before that dreadful day on Calvary flowed up to and was incorporated into that sacrificial death. This was the hidden meaning and the goal of all the centuries that passed before the event on Calvary's hill.

Jesus also foretold his forthcoming fate on the cross: "Just as Moses lifted up the serpent in the desert, so must the Son of Man be lifted up" (Jn 3:14).

All sanctifying experiences since the crucifixion are an outgrowth of the cross of Calvary. That cross gives meaning to life. It brings hope and reassurance. It is the source of strength and inspiration. It gives comfort and consolation.

Throughout the ages since the cross of Jesus was raised on Calvary, men and women have come in endless procession to rest in the shadow of the cross. "And I — once I am lifted up from the earth — will draw all men to myself" (Jn 12:32).

People of every walk and condition of life have come to rest in the shadow of the cross. Who are they?

Sinners

Sinners like ourselves come to the cross. As we linger in its shadow, we recall one of the many things that happened during those three eternal hours of warding off suffocation.

One of the criminals crucified with Jesus prayed: "Jesus, remember me when you enter upon your reign." Jesus did not ask for a confession or commitment, because he saw the criminal's heart. "I assure you," he promised, "this day you will be with me in paradise" (Lk 23:42–43).

Contemplation of this scene assures us that our sins are nailed to the cross. Jesus conquered sin and death and restored our relationship with the Father, never to be severed.

When we plead as the thief did, we can be certain of the same promise of being with Jesus in paradise.

The Dying

The dying lie at his feet in the shadow of the cross. They suffer the same fate Jesus suffered. Everyone must die. However, because of his death our death is the doorway into a community of perfect love. Our death is our entrance into the joy of heaven. In the shadow of the cross the dying find consolation and comfort as did St. Paul: "O death, where is your victory? O death, where is your sting?" (1 Cor 15:54–55)

Suffering

The suffering weep in the shadow of the cross. There is a secret locked into the mystery of suffering and pain. The suffering are tempted to discouragement, rebellion, even despair. However, in the shadow of the cross they find peace in spite of their pain. Here their tears can even be turned into joy.

In the shadow of the cross the suffering realize there is not a single pain which Jesus himself has not sanctified and made a stepping stone to perfect union with him.

They look beyond the cross, remembering that Jesus rose from the dead and is with them at every moment. The suffering find Jesus in the shadow of the cross, and there they find peace.

The Elderly

The elderly do not have much to look forward to in life, except that Jesus died to prepare the way for them. In the shadow of the cross they find a course of action which brings them comfort and joy.

The cross represents the total gift of Jesus in love to the Father for our redemption. This self-giving of Jesus gives them the generosity to say their yes to the Father also. Each day is a dying to self for them. In this process they are surrendering themselves in love to the Father, and with their giving of self, the Father is able to fill them more and more with his divine life.

In this gift of self, the elderly find peace and joy.

The Homeless

The homeless find refuge in the shadow of the cross. They kneel in the presence of that cross and understand that Jesus gave up everything to pave the way for them.

He was homeless. He could say, "The foxes have lairs, the birds in the sky have nests, but the Son of Man has nowhere to lay his head" (Mt 8:20).

Jesus gave up everything: his friends, his own garments, yes, even his Mother. He was abandoned by his own people, deserted by his disciples, betrayed by one, denied by another. He died outside the city, cut off from his own people.

Having given everything, he was the most homeless of the homeless.

The Lonely

How many suffer from the terrible disease of loneliness!

The lonely who kneel before Jesus in the shadow of the cross find great healing. As he was dying, he was the loneliest of men. He knew loneliness in the solitude of death. He experienced even apparent abandonment by his Father. "My God, my God, why have you forsaken me?" (Mt 27:46).

Jesus took all the bitterness of the lonely into his own heart because he has a special love for them. In the shadow of the cross, the lonely find their ordeal more tolerable and, in fact, begin to experience the peace of Jesus.

Lovers

Lovers come to the cross of Jesus, because in its shadow they find the greatest of all loves. "There is no greater love than this: to lay down one's life for one's friends" (Jn 15:13).

The warmth of this love radiating from the cross causes lovers to permit their own love to mature and burst into flame in spite of hardships and difficulties.

Genuine love must give. It must be translated into action. Nourished and fed by the unique love of Jesus, lovers can unselfishly give without counting the cost. They can give even joyously and graciously.

Children

Little ones come to kneel in the shadow of the cross. They may not understand all the implications of redemption, but in their own hearts they know that he loves them. Somehow they know that this was the price he paid for their happiness.

Jesus is pleased with their coming.

Father, Lord of heaven and earth, to you I offer praise; for what you have hidden from the learned and the clever you have revealed to the merest children. Father, it is true. You have graciously willed it so. (Mt 11:25-26)

Little ones come because they want to comfort Jesus and express their love in the shadow of the cross.

All of Us

All of us come to the cross. We can kneel. We can sit. We can rest in its shadow.

When our own cross seems heavy, when we are tempted to indulge in self-pity, we come and listen with our hearts as he says: "Come to me, all you who are weary and find life burdensome, and I will refresh you" (Mt 11:28).

We come when we are weary, because there is no other genuine source of comfort which can satisfy us, for he is "the God of all consolation! He comforts us in all our afflictions and thus enables us to comfort those who are in trouble, with the same consolation we have received from him." (2 Cor 1:3-4)

We come when we feel lonely and abandoned. We hear him crying out in his dying moment: "My God, my God, why have you forsaken me?" His plaintive cry reminds us that we are not alone. He is always with us.

We come when we have sinned. We come when we know that we have failed him.

We come when we are hurt, wounded, misunderstood, rejected.

We come when we find it hard to forgive and forget; when we are wronged, insulted, criticized.

As we sit in the shadow of his cross, we listen to all the insults, the ridicule, the blasphemy. Then above all the derision hurled at him, we hear loud and clear: "Father, forgive them; they do not know what they are doing" (Lk 23:34). Jesus not only asked forgiveness for his enemies, but he even excused them.

Pondering his words makes it easier for us to say: "Yes, I forgive."

We come to the cross of Jesus because it speaks more eloquently than words the message that every human heart longs to hear: "As the Father has loved me, so I have loved you" (Jn 15:9).

We wind our way to the cross on Calvary's hill because we hear Jesus say: "Yes, I love you just as you are. I don't care what you have done, I love you anyway."

And our heart sings: "Jesus, thank you for loving me! I love you too!"

NINE

Every Height Attained

Mary set out, proceeding in haste into the hill country.
(Lk 1:39)

GOD SEEMS TO DELIGHT in meeting his people on high places. In the course of man's salvific encounters with God, mountaintops and hills seem to be God's favorite trysting places.

One reason for this may be that when we are on a high mountain we can drink in the grandeur of the heavens and the expansive beauty of the earth. Consequently, we can more easily be aware of the presence of the Lord.

The second reason may be that on a height our vision is more panoramic and more cosmic. We more easily see beyond ourselves and our limited environment. We can better see God's plan of creation and his providential concern for all of it.

Annunciation

As Mother of Jesus and our Mother, Mary encountered God on various heights. Mary lived in Nazareth at the time of the Annunciation. Nazareth is built on a hill. When the inhabitants of Jesus' hometown rejected him, the height of Nazareth is mentioned: "They rose up and expelled him from the town, leading him to the brow of the hill on which it was built and intending to hurl him over the edge" (Lk 4:29).

Nazareth is 1230 feet above sea level, cupped in an amphitheater of hills.

Throughout her life Mary climbed many heights to meet God. Nazareth is the hallowed spot where the Incarnation took place.

Mary not only resided on the hill of Nazareth, but in her sinlessness she kept her heart and mind open and receptive to God at all times. Her abandonment to God's will and her commitment to him were total: "I am the servant of the Lord. Let it be done to me as you say." (Lk 1:38)

Like Mary, our attentiveness to the Lord walking with us and abiding within us will keep us aware of what God may be asking of us at any given moment. We, too, will encounter the Lord on the mystical mountain as we ascend in quiet, listening prayer.

Ain Karem

Immediately after this mysterious happening in Nazareth, Mary began another ascent. Mary did not conceive Jesus solely for herself. She was to present him to the world. She began this mission even before Jesus was born.

> Thereupon Mary set out, proceeding in haste into the hill country to a town in Judah, where she entered Zechariah's house and greeted Elizabeth. (Lk 1:39-40)

Notice again the mention of the "hill country."

Mary brought her unborn Son to Elizabeth and Zechariah and also to the unborn John here in the hill country of Judea.

> Elizabeth was filled with the Holy Spirit and cried out in a loud voice: "Blest are you among women and blest is the fruit of your womb. But who am I that the mother of my Lord should come to me? The moment your greeting sounded in my ears, the baby leapt in my womb for joy." (Lk 1:41-44)

Mary's response is preserved in her hymn of joy which the church prays daily and which begins:

> My being proclaims the greatness of the Lord, my spirit finds joy in God my savior. (Lk 1:46-47)

Mary introduces us to Jesus so that we may find hope and encouragement as we climb the mountains of the Lord during our earthly pilgrimage. Furthermore, the presence of Jesus reassures us that we never travel alone. He is treading every step of the way with us. He faithfully accompanies us to our own Emmaus. Our footsteps become lighter as he opens his Word to us and keeps "our hearts burning inside us" (Lk 24:32).

Bethlehem

Bethlehem, too, is situated on high ground. It is five miles south of Jerusalem on a hill 2600 feet above sea level. The surrounding hills are honeycombed with caves. One of these many caves became a natural cathedral as the angelic chorus chanted its celestial hymn of praise: "Glory to God in high heaven" (Lk 2:14).

What a mystery of love is hidden in John's poetic announcement: "The Word became flesh and made his dwelling among us, and we have seen his glory: the glory of an only Son coming from the Father, filled with enduring love" (Jn 1:14).

The mystery of the Incarnation is the greatest love story ever told. It is love translated into action. "Yes, God so loved the world that he gave his only Son, that whoever believes in him may not die but may have eternal life" (Jn 3:16).

Repeatedly we need to hear that we are loved. Yes, God so loved us that he gave us his only Son. Constantly we need to be reassured that we are lovable.

Every year in the liturgy of the church we climb the hill to Bethlehem's cave to find again the peace and joy which the Prince of Peace brings us. In the liturgical cycle Mary re-presents her Son to us — humble, needy, vulnerable, lying in a manger, but nevertheless the transcendent God of heaven and earth who pours out his infinite love upon us by becoming one of us. "He emptied himself . . . being born in the likeness of men" (Phil 2:7).

Our privilege is even greater. Christmas is not only an annual feast. At every eucharistic celebration Jesus is born again on our altars. Each day Mary leads us to Incarnate Love. Each day Jesus comes anew to dwell within us.

Presentation

In obedience to the Law of their people, Mary and Joseph climbed Mount Moriah and entered the temple of the Lord. There Mary presented her Son to the Lord, "for it is written in the Law of the Lord, 'Every first-born male shall be consecrated to the Lord' " (Lk 2:23).

Mary and Joseph could have claimed exemption from the law. Was not their Son the author of all law? Mary presented her Son in the temple to fulfill the prescriptions of the law and to give us an example.

This presentation brought joy and happiness to the saintly Simeon and Anna. Their persevering prayers to see the Messiah were fulfilled.

Once again Mary was reminded that God's ways are not our ways, nor are God's thoughts our thoughts. Simeon reminded Mary of the thorny path of rejection which lay ahead, since Jesus would not meet the erroneous expectations of a Messiah who would free his people from the domination of Rome and establish them as a great political power once again. They were looking for a Messiah who would restore the pristine glory of the Davidic reign. Mary's suffering would be so sharp that Simeon could say, "You yourself shall be pierced with a sword."

The Holy Family prepared the way for us. Our life is a continuous surrendering in love to God by dying to ourselves each day in all the circumstances of life. This is the price of discipleship. This is the privilege of love.

Calvary

Calvary is a hill of contradiction. It is the height of shame, degradation, rejection, and failure. At the same time, the greatest victory ever achieved in human history was gained here.

Walk with Mary as she silently and sorrowfully presents her Son along that bloodstained way of the cross. Every step was a renewed act of love, a response to the Father. Jesus explained: "The Father loves me for this: that I lay down my life to take it up again" (Jn 10:17).

Jesus not only laid down his life to prove his love for us, but he took it up again to manifest that same love, because now he lives within us in his resurrected life. Mary would also bid us listen as Jesus says: "There is no greater love than this: to lay down one's life for one's friends" (Jn 15:13).

A mystery is hidden in the darkness which "came over the whole land" (Lk 23:44). It is the mystery of Love—infinite Love.

Mary, too, gave herself without reserve: "Near the cross of Jesus, there stood his mother" (Jn 19:25). Mary's posture of standing is significant. It indicates the fathomless love which bound the hearts of Jesus and Mary. They were as one in making their oblation to the Father.

Mary presents her Son who makes the total gift of himself to the Father in our name. Each day in the eucharist we are privileged to unite ourselves to the gift of Jesus so that his image may be formed in us and we may become a gift pleasing and acceptable to our Father.

As we closely follow Jesus in our daily living, we are transformed into his image. This is the gift of ourselves which the Father desires.

To accomplish it, we must walk our own way to Calvary and there let Jesus help us to die to self and put on his image.

The Cenacle

Mary made another significant climb. After Jesus ascended into heaven she returned to ascend Mount Zion once again to the Upper Room, the Cenacle. Here Mary is found with the apostles in fervent prayer, pleading for the church born in the outpouring of the Holy Spirit. "Together they devoted themselves to constant prayer. There were some women in their company, and Mary the mother of Jesus, and his brothers." (Act 1:14).

As the Mother of the Church, Mary was here at its birth. Mary became the Mother of the Church at the moment she conceived Jesus, the Head of the Church. On Calvary Jesus formally presented her to the church, represented by St. John: "There is your mother" (Jn 19:27).

In the Cenacle atop Mount Zion, Mary exercises her maternal

prerogative as she presents Jesus, risen and gloriously reigning, in the fullness of the Spirit being poured out upon the church.

Mary constantly prays for us, that we may be receptive and cooperative with the outpouring of the Spirit.

Dormition

If you were to visit the Holy Land today you would discover on Mount Zion an imposing structure called the Basilica of the Dormition. According to one tradition this marks the site where Mary's earthly life ended and from which she entered heaven. This beautiful church was built in 1919 by the Benedictine Fathers.

Mary climbed Mount Zion for the last time. How she longed to be free of this mortal coil and be reunited with her Divine Son! According to God's plan she was to mother the infant church with all her maternal wisdom and love. Even though her will was perfectly in accord with God's will, nevertheless she awaited the day when she would enter the eternal bliss of heaven.

There is a question today whether or not Mary actually died as do the rest of us mortals. Some believe that she simply went to sleep and was taken bodily into heaven. The word sleep is used frequently in scripture meaning death; hence this does not clarify the problem.

A second school of thought teaches that Mary, like any other human person, had to die as do all mortals. Soon after her death her incorrupt body was taken into heaven.

The formal teaching of the church does not clarify the matter. In his encyclical *Munificentissimus Deus*, Pope Pius XII said: "The Immaculate Mother of God, the ever-Virgin Mary, *having completed the course of her earthly life*, was assumed body and soul into heavenly glory."

The words, "having completed the course of her earthly life," give us no hint whether or not Mary died or simply was bodily glorified without dying.

After Jesus' ascension, Mary's life on earth was somewhat of an exile. She was happy to remain on earth to nurture and encourage the infant church, but she longed to be with her Son. Love always seeks presence.

Mary's sinlessness afforded her an expanded consciousness of the joy and richness of the love of God. Her heart burned to be with her Son. She would have welcomed death.

We fear death, because of its unknown factor. We cling tenaciously to life, because we cannot comprehend the happiness awaiting us.

Eagerly and expectantly Mary climbed that last mountain from which she figuratively took her flight into heaven and into the arms of her Divine Son.

Speaking metaphorically we can visualize Mary standing on the threshold of heaven, eagerly awaiting our arrival into that joy and peace which the world cannot give.

Jesus came into the world through Mary. She is now united with him in heaven. And as we look forward to our entry into glory we pray:

Holy Mary, Mother of God,
pray for us sinners now and
at the hour of our death.

TEN

The Lord's Mountain

He carried me away in spirit to the top of a very high mountain. (Rv 21:10)

ON OUR JOURNEY through life we are approaching our climb up the last and most important mountain. Our pilgrimage is steadily advancing toward our total union with our loving Father in heaven. Each day brings us closer to that doorway which admits us into "the kingdom prepared for you from the creation of the world" (Mt 25:34). Our insatiable curiosity makes us frequently wonder what heaven must be like. We wonder what we will experience on the top of that final mountain toward which we journey.

Sacred scripture tells us little about heaven. Jesus did not come to give us a detailed description about life after life. Our finite minds could not comprehend it anyway. Jesus came into the world to teach us how to live each day in order to reach our home with him in glorious bliss of heaven.

Even though St. Paul had visions and revelations to the extent that he was caught up in the outer fringes, he was unable to verbalize clearly what he had experienced. In floundering for a verbal description of his vision, he merely quoted the prophet Isaiah: "Eye has not seen, ear has not heard, nor has it so much as dawned on man what God has prepared for those who love him" (1 Cor 2:9).

In speaking of his own experience, Paul, in his humility, speaks of it as happening to some other person: "I know that this man . . . was snatched up to Paradise to hear words which cannot be uttered, words which no man may speak" (2 Cor 12:3-4). Paul could not find words with which to relate his "otherworldly" experience. Even though Paul could not express his experience in words, his pastoral zeal does not prevent him from encouraging us to keep our focus on heaven, our true home.

> Since you have been raised up in company with Christ, set your heart on what pertains to higher realms where Christ is seated at God's right hand. Be intent on things above rather than on things of earth. After all, you have died! Your life is hidden now with Christ in God. When Christ our life appears, then you shall appear with him in glory. (Col 3:1-4)

This pastoral admonition from St. Paul may seem difficult until we remember that our loving Father is eagerly awaiting our entry into heaven with him. Furthermore, he is anxious to help us over any difficulties. The psalmist also assures us, "When I call out to the Lord, he answers me from his holy mountain" (Ps 3:5).

While we have no direct or detailed revelation about what heaven will be like, it is surprising how much we do actually know about life after death. From the implications of what Jesus taught, from the constant traditions of the church, and from the insights of the saints and mystics, we can glean considerable knowledge about heaven.

We know that we will love and be loved with an unfathomable and ever-increasing love. We will be continually overwhelmed by God's beauty and goodness. While we will be perfectly content, we will continue to thirst for more and more.

We shall see God "face to face" (1 Cor 13:12). Each one of us will be known and loved by God in the most intimate way possible. He will give himself totally to each one of us.

We will be perfectly happy and secure in this eternal happiness, knowing that there is no possibility of ever losing it. Jesus assures us that heaven goes on forever and ever. It is eternal. Speaking of reward and punishment after judgment, Jesus says: "These will go off to eternal punishment and the just to eternal life" (Mt 25:46).

When Paul explains the glorification of the body, he teaches that our bodies will be incorruptible and immortal—"this corruptible body must be clothed with incorruptibility, this mortal body with immortality" (1 Cor 15:53).

In this heavenly state there will be no sorrow, no pain, no hardship.

> He shall dwell with them and they shall be his people and he shall be their God who is always with them. He shall wipe every tear from their eyes, and there shall be no more death or mourning, crying out or pain, for the former world has passed away. (Rv 21:3–4)

We will enjoy full knowledge. We will understand the mysteries of our faith which now baffle us. We will know the secrets of the universe.

Heaven is continuous growth. God's love for us is infinite. We shall never be able to exhaust it. We open more and more to his love in heaven and his love within us is intensified.

This process will also affect our consciousness. Even now we know how our consciousness can be expanded as we acquire more and more knowledge. In heaven it will be expanded to the extent that we will be fully ourselves, aware to the depth of our being. We will have perfect love for and friendship with others.

Heaven is really living at last. It is a continual growth in knowledge and love, an endless expanding of our whole being, while enjoying perfect peace.

In heaven we shall know those we have known and loved on this earth. We will delight in one another's perfection and in our mutual love. We will not be distracted and turn away from God. Rather, we will see God clearly in all things, acting through them, giving himself and revealing himself through them. Everything will be sacred, for God is "all in all."

> I tell you again and again, my brethren, that in the Lord's garden are to be found not only the rose of his martyrs. In it there are also the lilies of the virgins, the ivy of wedded couples, and the violets of the widows. On no account may any class or people despair, thinking that God has not called them. Christ suffered for all. What the Scriptures say of him is true: "He

desires all men to be saved and to come to knowledge of the truth." (St. Augustine, Sermon 304, 1-4)

The Bible pictures eternal life with images of activity and celebration. It often speaks of the banquet of the Lord as a festive, joyous celebration. Because we have been faithful in little things during our life on earth, we will enjoy not only the Lord's joy but all his good things and be more responsibly active and involved in this world and the universe (Mt 25:21; Lk 19:17, 19).

New Universe

We more and more realize that none of us will fully arrive at the mountaintop of heaven until we all arrive. In some mysterious way we are all bound together, dependent upon one another, so that in helping another person we are ultimately helping ourselves. The scripture and also some of the concepts of Vatican Council II make us more aware of the fact that we are a people on a journey toward our final destiny. Paul teaches that we form one inter-dependent Body of Christ.

St. Peter assures us that in the end there will be a new universe —a new heaven and a new earth: "What we await are new heavens and a new earth where, according to his promise, the justice of God will reside" (2 Pt 3:13).

Since the material world has suffered from the disorder that has come from sin, it is only fitting that it should share in our final glory. This is Paul's conviction:

Creation was made subject to futility, not of its own accord but by him who once subjected it; yet not without hope, because the world itself will be freed from its slavery to corruption and share in the glorious freedom of the children of God. Yes, we know that all creation groans and is in agony even until now. Not only that, but we ourselves, although we have the Spirit as first fruits, groan inwardly while we await the redemption of our bodies. (Rom 8:20-23)

The universe will be beautiful and perfect beyond our imagining. We do not know the exact nature of this perfect universe, but we do know that nature will be in harmony with itself and with God. There will be no more destructive storms, devastating tornadoes, earthquakes, floods, etc. There will be a vast cosmic renewal and glorification of God as he will be revealed in all things.

We have a role to play in this gigantic renewal. God has created the world and placed an unfinished universe in our hands. He has entrusted to us the privilege of perfecting his work. Every step we take toward harnessing nature, toward using its potential, implements creation and carries out God's plan of love. We are "co-creators" with God. The more we keep ourselves aware of this responsibility, the more we contribute, particularly by reaching out in love to others.

As Christians we have a great responsibility and a rare privilege, as we fulfill our role toward helping perfect the universe. We can never be satisfied with things as they are. Every conquest of nature must serve to radiate love, not tyranny. A loving touch in our own environment will contribute to the perfection of all things.

As we persevere in our mountain climbing throughout life, we are aware that God has a meaningful plan and purposeful end in all that happens. We know that one day all things will be perfected in Christ. We know that none of our efforts will ever be wasted. Everything is in God's inscrutable plan.

We may fail at times, hurt our fellowman, neglect to reach out in love to others, but we know that a compassionate God will forgive and welcome us at the height of our final mountain.

In a letter to Proba, St. Augustine writes encouragingly:

The deeper our faith, the stronger our hope, the greater our desire, the larger will be our capacity to receive that gift, which is very great indeed. No eye has seen it; it has no color. No ear has heard it; it has no sound. It has not entered man's heart; man's heart must enter it.

When the Apostle tells us: "Pray without ceasing," he means this: Desire unceasingly that life of happiness which is nothing if not eternal, and ask it of him who alone is able to give it.

(Ep 130,8,15,17)

We are convinced that Jesus really meant it when he said, "I solemnly assure you, the man who hears my word and has faith in him who sent me possesses eternal life" (Jn 5:24). With St. Paul we can say, "We groan while we are here, even as we yearn to have our heavenly habitation envelop us" (2 Cor 5:2). Furthermore, even though we may see obscurely now, our faith convinces us "that neither death nor life, neither angels nor principalities, neither the present nor the future, nor powers, neither height nor depth nor any other creature, will be able to separate us from the love of God that comes to us in Christ Jesus, our Lord" (Rom 8:38–39).

Trudging those final miles on our ascent to God's holy mountain, our steps become lighter and lighter. We are drawn by the magnetic power of his divine love.

Our hearts cry out in ecstatic joy: "Come, Lord Jesus!" (Rv 22:20).